Born in Adelaide in 1974, Jeremy Pudney was also raised in the South Australian capital. He completed a Journalism degree at the University of South Australia and began his journalism career in 1993.

Jeremy was a police reporter at South Australia's only daily newspaper, *The Advertiser*, when the Snowtown murders story broke. He is now a television reporter with Network Ten in Melbourne. Primarily a police reporter, he is also assigned to major national and international stories.

The Bodies in the Barrels Murders is Jeremy's first book.

THE BODIES
IN THE BARRELS
MURDERS

THEY TORTURED AND KILLED TWELVE PEOPLE
THIS IS THEIR TRUE STORY

JEREMY PUDNEY

JOHN BLAKE

Published By John Blake Publishing Ltd,
3, Bramber Court, 2 Bramber Road,
London W14 9PB, England

www.blake.co.uk

First published in Australia in 2005 by HarperCollins Publishers (Australia) Pty
Limited Group. This edition published by arrangement with HarperCollins.
First published in paperback in the UK in 2006

ISBN 1 84454 207 6

British Library Cataloguing-in-Publication Data:

A catalogue record for this book is available from the British Library.

Design by www.envydesign.co.uk

Printed and bound in Great Britain by Bookmarque

1 3 5 7 9 10 8 6 4 2

Papers used by John Blake Publishing are natural, recyclable products made from wood
grown in sustainable forests. The manufacturing processes conform to the environmental
regulations of the country of origin.

Every attempt has been made to contact the relevant copyright-holders, but some were
unavailable. We would be grateful if the appropriate people could contact us.

Names marked * have been changed.

*This book is dedicated to the
police who bring killers to justice.*

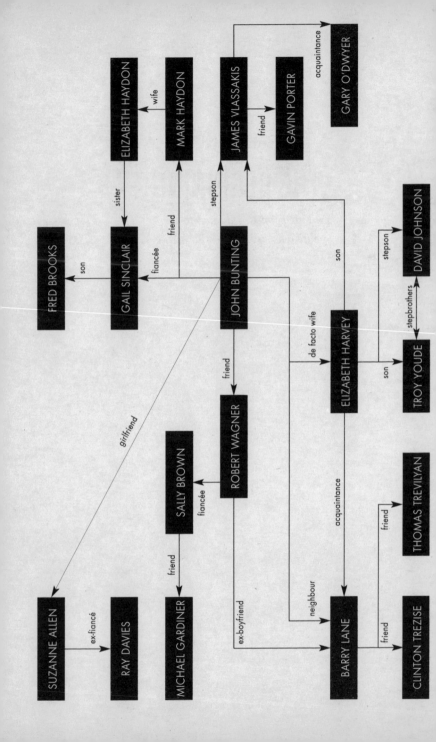

PART ONE

THE BEGINNING

ONE

There is something alluring about the city of Adelaide. Few other cities in the world possess such a unique and charming mix of handsome historic buildings, wide streets, cosmopolitan cafés and an abundance of beautiful parks and gardens. The air is clean, the lifestyle enjoyable and the people friendly. It's even safe to walk the streets at night. At least for the most part.

Adelaide's central business district has no serious skyscrapers to speak of, and covers what's lovingly called 'the square mile'. Beyond it the city's suburbs sprawl out in every direction, hemmed in by the picturesque Adelaide Hills to the east and a spectacular, pristine coastline to the west.

National Highway One cuts a swathe through Adelaide's northern suburbs and, beyond the urban sprawl, continues further north through barren, lonely country. As its journey continues towards South Australia's wheat belt, known as the Mid North, there is little more than salt-encrusted lands to one side of the highway and sun-scorched paddocks to the other.

Along the highway, 150 kilometres from Adelaide, is the small hamlet of Snowtown. It is a town nestled in the heart of a farming district noted for its quality stock breeding, fat lambs, wool and wheat crops. Settlers had come to the region in the 1840s seeking pastures for their flocks, and settled the town in 1867.

In the past few decades Snowtown has become, like many settlements in the Australian bush, a town in decay. Economically times are tough and, while the population is just over 500, it tends to fluctuate as local young people leave to look for work or, simply, a better life. Others trickle in from Adelaide, lured by cheap housing and the rural lifestyle. Snowtown's appearance is evidence of a past boom time: its wide main street is virtually deserted during the day and the town is dissected by a rail line on which trains that used to stop now barely slow as they pass.

Thursday, 20 May 1999, was an unseasonably warm day and Detectives Greg Stone and Steve McCoy hardly noticed the 'Welcome to Snowtown' sign as their unmarked police car cruised into town. Their minds were on a job that for the past six months had led the pair on the trail of a group they now suspected were serial killers. Five people had vanished in four years; all were presumed murdered and cash had been siphoned from some of their bank accounts. There were at least three suspects, but no bodies had been found. Detectives at the South Australia Police Major Crime Branch had been on the case for almost two years.

Investigations were well advanced and the evidence was mounting. A crucial piece in the puzzle, however, had not been found. Six months ago, just after a woman named Elizabeth Haydon had vanished, a witness reported seeing an old Toyota four-wheel drive parked outside one of the suspects' houses in Adelaide's northern suburbs. Late one afternoon, the witness noticed a man loading plastic garbage bags into the vehicle. She described the back of the vehicle as being stacked from the 'floor to the roof', saying,

'The man needed to push and force the bags into the rear of the Land Cruiser.'

By the time police learned of this suspicious cargo, the four-wheel drive had vanished.

Detectives Stone and McCoy arrived at the Snowtown police station at 11.30 a.m. and within minutes a team of officers had gathered inside. With them were Major Crime detectives Jane Dickinson and Mark Wilson, local investigator Rick Day, Senior Constable Ian Young and three crime scene examiners: Gordon Drage, Andrew Bosley and Bronwyn Marsh. Their assignment, they were told, was to search a house at 25 Railway Terrace, Snowtown. They were to look carefully for anything that might be linked to the five missing persons; in particular, property and bank documents.

Most importantly, they were to examine and seize a vehicle in the driveway of the house. It was the Toyota Land Cruiser police had been hunting, which had been spotted there four days earlier.

The first thing Simon Jones★ noticed was the line of cars pulling up outside his house. They included the local policeman's wagon, followed by a tilt-tray truck. Next came the knock at the door; the detective who spoke first flipped open his wallet to display his police badge.

'I'm Detective Senior Constable Steve McCoy.' He introduced the other officers. 'We've been investigating the disappearance of a woman named Elizabeth Haydon and we believe that a four-wheel drive may have been or was involved in that disappearance. We need to speak to you about the four-wheel drive in your driveway.'

McCoy showed Jones a search warrant and explained that his home would be searched and the vehicle seized.

The detective then led Jones to a police car out the front, where he would be interviewed.

As some of the officers began scouring the inside of Jones's home, filming their search with a video camera, Detective Stone made his way to the four-wheel drive. His eyes pored over the vehicle, which was mostly empty. He noticed that the registration plates had been removed and three windows had been left down.

Sitting in the police car, McCoy began questioning Jones about the four-wheel drive. Confused and a little frightened, Jones explained that the vehicle was not his but had been towed to his house by two friends. The friends' names were recognised instantly by McCoy – they were two of the suspects.

Inside the broken-down four-wheel drive, Jones's friends had apparently stored several large black plastic barrels. They had emitted such a foul odour that his neighbours had complained.

'Where are the barrels now?'

As McCoy asked the question, Jones turned and gestured.

'They're over in the bank.'

McCoy stopped the interview, got out of the car and approached his colleagues.

'I think we've found the bodies.'

It was precisely 1.12 p.m. when Detectives McCoy and Stone, along with officers Drage, Marsh and Day, arrived at the old bank. It was a plain red-brick building, nothing much to look at except for the imposing steel front doors, which had been closed by bank staff for the last time some four years earlier.

The police passed through a gate and approached the

bank's side door. Simon Jones had given them a key – Jones's friends had leased the bank and left the key with him. In fact, he said, they'd even allowed him to store equipment from his electronics business inside the building.

Detective Day opened the side door and the officers moved in; Drage was first through the door and was using a video camera to record their every move. Just inside was a kitchen area, and a door to the right leading to the bank proper. The bank counter and much of the customer area were stacked with cardboard boxes, each packed with computer parts, other electronics and an assortment of junk. Televisions and computer monitors in various states of repair were scattered around the floor.

Drage noticed a plastic shopping bag hanging from a door near the counter, filled with rubbish including a receipt. The docket detailed the purchase of air fresheners, rubber gloves and garbage bags. An air freshener was operating from a power point in the room, and a brief search of cupboards at the back of the counter uncovered several unused garbage bags.

The officers then turned their attention to the large, cream-coloured vault door. It was locked. Close examination of the door revealed the presence of a fingerprint in the top left-hand corner and Drage dusted the print with black powder, highlighting its swirling outline. The fingerprint needed to be photographed, so Drage headed back to Simon Jones's house to collect his other camera. While there, the officer mentioned to one of his colleagues that the vault door was locked. No problem, Simon Jones told him. He knew how to open it.

As he led Drage to a large coil of galvanised fencing wire, Jones explained that the tumbler lock on the vault door didn't work and the door could be opened with a piece of wire. Jones cut off a length of wire and used a pair of pliers to make a small bend at one end and a larger turn at the other.

Drage returned to the bank and apprehensively pushed the wire into the lock. Crouched at the door, it took him only a few seconds of manipulation before he could feel that a tumbler inside the lock was moving. A little pressure and the vault door's chrome handle shifted to the unlocked position.

At 2.24 p.m. Drage pressed the record button on the police video camera, its lens pointed towards the vault door. Detective Stone, wearing surgical gloves so as not to contaminate vital forensic evidence, reached for the handle and the heavy door swung open.

Black plastic sheeting covered the entrance, with clear adhesive tape securing it to the inside of the doorframe. A long vertical slit had been cut down the centre of the sheeting, obviously to allow access to the vault, and this too had been sealed with tape.

In the recess between the vault door and the plastic the officers noticed a wallet, a roll of packing tape, two keys and a book of lined writing paper.

As Stone peeled back the single strip of tape from the top – breaking the seal – he recoiled at the pungent smell emanating from the vault. There was no mistaking the stench of rotting remains.

Stone prised the plastic apart and, clasping his police-issue torch, quickly scanned the inside of the vault. He forced the plastic further apart and took a step inside, followed by Drage, his camera still rolling.

The two officers had stepped into a place that had been the scene of unspeakable acts. It was dark, the stench overpowering, and they had yet to fully comprehend the gravity of their discovery. To their right were six large plastic barrels, each black and sealed with a screw-top lid. They may not have been able to see inside, but neither Stone nor Drage doubted that each of these barrels contained human remains.

The barrels stood on two large pieces of black plastic positioned as drop sheets. On top of one barrel was a sinister sign: a pair of silver handcuffs and, next to them, a black-handled knife. On top of another barrel were two more black-handled knives and a pair of green rubber gloves.

To the officers' left, against the vault's northern wall, was a pale green lounge chair on which sat a white plastic tray containing seven more knives. Alongside were two boxes of disposable gloves, a wooden-handled saw and what looked like a belt. In the back left corner of the small room was another lounge chair with three white plastic bottles, each bearing a label which read 'Hydrochloric Acid'. Scanning the inside of the vault, the officers could make out an array of other items − a can of air freshener, a pair of sandshoes and a scattering of garbage bags, some of them full.

Outside the bank Steve McCoy made a telephone call to the Major Crime office in Adelaide. He reported that human bodies had been found, but exactly how many − and who they were − was unclear. McCoy then returned to the bank and gave the order to clear the building. By 2.30 p.m. the side door was closed and a guard stationed outside.

The cavalry was coming.

TWO

John Bunting liked to watch them die, to see how quickly the chemical would devour them. He delighted in every convulsion. Sometimes their bodies disintegrated altogether. Trapping his prey was easy; any insect would do, although his favourite catch was one of the redback spiders living under his house. Bunting would drop them into different chemicals – brake fluid, hydrochloric acid, nitric acid or even chlorine – taking careful note as to which was the most efficient at killing. Then he would use it again. This was the darker side of a boy who otherwise seemed typical for his age. It was also a sign of the evil to come.

John Justin Bunting was born on 4 September 1966 in the Australian east-coast city of Brisbane, the capital of Queensland. The inner-city suburb of Inala, where Bunting spent his childhood, was a stark contrast to Queensland's golden, tropical image. It was a working-class district characterised by high crime and soaring unemployment rates, public housing and a large number of migrant families.

Bunting's parents, Jan and Tom, doted on their only child and gave him as much as their meagre income would allow. Their son seemed to be a normal, curious lad and his early years were spent drifting from one hobby to the next, as so many teenage boys did. There was astronomy, electronics and photography.

With young friend Kurt Bertrand, Bunting would make trips to the museum or art gallery and take photographs. The pair would even photograph the moon through a telescope; all their pictures were developed with chemicals stored in the makeshift darkroom Bunting's parents had let him create at home. Indeed, it was from these innocent beginnings that his more sinister interest in chemicals would stem. Bunting had wanted to study both chemistry and physics at Inala High School, but because he hadn't studied advanced mathematics, he wasn't allowed.

There was also Bunting's bizarre obsession with digging. During one school holiday he and Kurt carved out an elaborate tunnel under Bunting's home. It was almost 4 metres underground, 5 metres long and, inside, about 1.5 metres high. The boys braced the walls with wood and bricks, Bunting hoping they would be able to tunnel under the back yard and create an underground room. The project came to an abrupt end when Tom Bunting discovered the tunnel and demanded it be filled in.

Yet another source of fascination for Bunting was weaponry. As a young teen he would extract gunpowder from fireworks to make rocket mortars; sometimes he mixed his own gunpowder. The excitement of shooting at targets with a slug gun eventually led to Bunting acquiring a collection of more powerful rifles and shotguns. As well, his interest in weapons attracted him to books about World War II, which in turn introduced him to the philosophies of Nazism and white supremacy. As a young adult Bunting made contact with a neo-Nazi group in Sydney and obtained a copy of Adolf Hitler's book *Mein Kampf*. He tried unsuccessfully to buy a Nazi flag and an SS uniform, even painting a Nazi swastika inside the boot of his first car. His mother discovered the disturbing mural and promptly painted over it.

Bunting's racist and homophobic views gained momentum with his interest in Nazism. What began as a strong dislike became a burning hatred, particularly for homosexuals and paedophiles. In his mind there was little difference between the two. During conversations with friends, Bunting would rant about knowing where 'fairies' or 'poofters' lived. Eventually he would speak of going out and bashing them, although no one ever saw anything to suggest his talk was more than just that. What Bunting's friends didn't know was that there was a far more deep-seated, albeit irrational, explanation for his hate.

Later in life Bunting would tell those close to him of a time when he and a young friend were beaten and sexually assaulted by the friend's older brother. The prolonged attack ended only when the boy's father came home. The teenager then took off on his motorbike and was killed in a crash. Bunting, who was only about eight years old at the time, claimed to have never told his parents.

There was another secret, too, that Bunting would tell only to those close to him. At age fifteen he'd had a brief encounter with a girl who became pregnant and later gave birth to a baby named Tammy. Bunting rarely visited the child and eventually lost contact altogether. He would almost never speak of his daughter and, from that time on, became involved in few relationships. As a young man, John Bunting had many friends but was close to no one.

After completing Year 11 at school, Bunting drifted from one menial job to the next. The first was with a sign-writing business; the next was travelling Australia to erect and repair nets at indoor sports centres. After being retrenched, Bunting moved out of home and into a shared house with friends. Kurt was among them, as was another longtime friend named Mark Day.

'The thing that really stood out about John Bunting is that he didn't try and big-note [talk up] himself, he was very down-to-earth and he didn't lie to make himself look better than he was,' Day would later tell police. 'He was just a genuinely nice bloke and I liked that about him.'

Bunting's final job before leaving Queensland was at a crematorium.

It was Mark Day's idea to leave the unemployment and depression that had engulfed him in Inala. He and John had become friends, spending hours together working on cars, and Bunting was quick to agree that he would also make the journey to Western Australia. The road trip began in February 1986 with seven adults, three children, two cars and hundreds of kilometres of highway. It came to a premature end when one of the cars broke down in Adelaide, South Australia.

With their adventure cut short, Bunting, Mark and his girlfriend, Esmay Kennedy, were quickly plunged back into reality. At first they lived in an Adelaide caravan park, then in a flat north of the city. When Esmay lost the baby she'd been expecting, she and Mark returned to Queensland, leaving Bunting to move into yet another caravan park.

Despite never reaching Western Australia, life in Adelaide was starting to take shape for John Bunting. In 1988 he got a temporary job working at a motor museum where his task was to help paint a concrete floor in the museum's main pavilion. Colleagues remember Bunting as an average-looking man, if a little short. He had shoulder-length, sandy-coloured hair and looked a touch younger than his twenty-one years. Their most vivid memory was of his voice. 'He had an unusually squeaky, high-pitched voice. It was almost as though his voice was breaking during the time he was employed by the museum,' one staff member would later recall.

Bunting's workmates also remembered his 'wild claims as to being able to steal power tools to order'. He spoke of taking part in 'ram raids' but those around him dismissed the stories as Bunting simply big-noting himself.

Nonetheless Bunting was a valued employee who was dismissed only because there wasn't enough money to keep him. A reference written for Bunting when he left the museum's employ described him as a 'very diligent, willing and intelligent worker, who carried out the work required of him in a thorough and enthusiastic manner'.

By late 1988 Bunting was living in a house in Adelaide's northern suburbs which he was sharing with friend Kevin Reid and Kevin's then partner, Michelle White. Kevin worked at the nearby SA Meat Corporation and managed to get Bunting some casual work there. Company records indicate that at first Bunting worked at the abattoir's 'southern works beef hall'. Employees were required to have basic knife skills for working at the evisceration table, where a beast's liver, spleen and other intestinal areas were sliced out for offal production. Later he was shifted to the by-products area, where a general labourer such as Bunting would spend his shift bagging meat meal or on general rendering duties. It was horrid, bloody work but John Bunting seemed to enjoy it. Every afternoon he would come home stinking of the putrid slaughterhouse odour but not be aware of it, because a childhood illness had robbed him of his sense of smell. While there is no record of John Bunting's duties having included the actual slaughter of animals, he would often brag that this was the part of his job he enjoyed most. Sitting at the dinner table, Bunting would describe how he used a stun gun to immobilise an animal before cutting its throat.

In the time they shared the house with him, both Kevin and Michelle witnessed Bunting's darker side first-hand. He spoke openly of his hatred of homosexuals and paedophiles and still seemed unable to differentiate between the two. On one occasion Bunting spoke of a man he knew to be a convicted paedophile and how he planned to bash him with an iron bar.

Michelle, in particular, found John Bunting to be a strange and frightening man. 'I can remember him reading things on making your own ... poisons and what they do,' she said later. 'He had guns, big guns, shotguns, some had magazines on them. He kept them under his bed. I remember he bought a petrol blowtorch. I remember him playing in the back garden with it.'

Another time Kevin discovered – in the ceiling above the laundry – a selection of items including a bottle of poison, rope, a balaclava and a knife with a long, curved blade. He and Michelle had planned to report it to the police but Bunting objected.

Michelle also recalls the time Bunting decided to kill Kevin's bull terrier dog because it had attacked his blue heeler. 'About lunchtime John came round to see me and asked me to come out to the shed as he wanted to show me something. I asked him what it was. He told me it was Kevin's dog – he had killed it and it was hanging in the shed.'

Later she watched from the kitchen window as Bunting dragged the dog, in a green plastic bag, to his car. Before Bunting drove off the pair decided to tell Kevin the dog had run away. When he returned, the lower left leg on his jeans was torn. 'I had some trouble,' Bunting explained. 'It was lying on the floor of the front passenger side and it woke up and started to attack me while I was driving.' Bunting told her he had kept kicking the dog as he tried to control the car, eventually booting the animal from the vehicle and taking off.

Even long after moving from the shared house, Michelle encountered John Bunting's mean streak as she spoke of an ex-boyfriend she was having trouble with. 'You know, I could do him in if you like,' John told her, before demonstrating how he could use chlorophyll to render a person unconscious.

It was during a slow period at the abattoir in January 1989 that John Bunting undertook a metalwork course which involved on-site training at a factory. It was here he met the eighteen-year-old woman who would become his wife. Veronika Tripp was a fragile, dependent teenager who lived at home with her parents. She had been completely deaf until undergoing surgery at eight years of age, and her vision was poor. Veronika also suffered intellectual difficulties and was barely literate.

At the beginning of their relationship the couple would go out on regular dates. Sometimes Bunting would take his new girlfriend for rides on his motorbike, at other times to the movies. 'We used to go to the pictures together,' Veronika said recently, 'and saw mainly horror films, as that was what John wanted to see. I never got to pick the pictures, he always did. He liked movies with blood and guts, war movies and people being shot.'

After her nineteenth birthday Veronika moved into the house Bunting shared with Kevin and Michelle. It was here that Veronika became acquainted with Bunting's aggressive nature when they argued. 'He never got actually physical with me but used to throw objects at me like plastic cups and plates.'

In September 1989, the pair were married at the local registry office but continued to live in the house they shared with Kevin and Michelle.

John and Veronika Bunting's first home together was a government-owned rental house in one of Adelaide's poorest northern suburbs. The address was 203 Waterloo Corner Road, Salisbury North. Records show the couple began renting the semi-attached house on 14 December 1991.

THREE

Robert Joe Wagner was only seven years old when he tried to kill himself. He took an overdose of his mother's sleeping pills.

In the months beforehand, Wagner's mother had noticed a dramatic change in her son. He had become quiet and introverted, and seemed to shy away from teenage males. Wagner would not tell his mother what was troubling him, nor would he speak to a psychologist. It was only after the failed suicide bid that his mother learned the truth: a teenage family friend had sexually abused her son.

Until the abuse Wagner had been a normal child, in the words of his mother, 'one minute mischievous, one minute naughty and the next minute lovable'. Born in New South Wales on 28 November 1971, he was only six months old when his father walked out of his life, leaving him and his older sister to be raised by their mother. Wagner was three when the family moved to Adelaide's northern suburbs.

The abuse had a profound effect on Robert Wagner. He would never be the same. At school he struggled to learn even basic reading and writing and was held back for an extra year in primary school. He started high school in 1984 but would regularly skip classes and often not turn up to school at all. By the end of his first year the school had given in to his truancy and he was allowed to stay home. At thirteen years old, and with little to occupy his time, Wagner would disappear from home for days in a row, his worried mother regularly reporting him missing to police. During one of these absences some of Wagner's young friends told his mother that her son had been spending time at a stranger's house in a neighbouring suburb.

Eventually Wagner took his mother to meet this stranger he'd befriended. To her horror, her son introduced her to a transvestite calling himself Vanessa Lane. The man's real name was Barry Lane; he was a paedophile. Using gifts to lure Wagner, Lane had taken a physical and psychological grip on the teenager and, despite his mother's pleas, Wagner refused to stop seeing Lane. The following year, when Wagner was fourteen and Lane thirty-one, the pair disappeared. Wagner's mother reported her son missing but heard nothing for four years.

Barry Lane led a bizarre and perverse life. He was a predator who, ultimately, would become the prey.

Born Barry Wayne Venables on 7 August 1955, he was a sickly baby. Suspecting that he was malnourished, child welfare authorities took him from his parents when he was eight months old. After a short stint in foster care Lane's grandmother won custody of him, raising her grandson in the rural town of Port Pirie, SA, where his mother also lived. Lane was given what outsiders described as a 'good Christian upbringing', but his childhood compulsion to dress up in girls' clothing worried his grandmother.

By the time he was sixteen, Lane was openly homosexual and pursuing sexual relationships with other teenage boys. At one point, concerned he had upset his grandmother, Lane attempted a relationship with a girl named Kathy. It quickly ended.

At seventeen, Lane left home and travelled Australia, living in Sydney, Melbourne and then Adelaide. He was employed for a period as a gardener but had little full-time work and eventually went onto a disability pension after apparently suffering a back injury.

While Lane maintained contact with his family, his relationship with his mother was strained. Perhaps unable to accept his sexuality, Sylvia Lane believed he was not her real son. Her child, she suspected, had been 'mixed up' with another baby when he was taken into foster care.

As a young man Barry Lane grappled with sexual confusion and perversion. He felt he wanted to be a woman, and to that end became a transvestite. He would wear women's clothing, carry a handbag and insist on being called Vanessa or Kim. He even took hormones to stimulate breast growth and reduce body hair.

Lane also harboured sexual desires towards young boys. In 1980, having previously fronted court on similar charges, Lane was sentenced to four months' jail after being convicted of indecently assaulting two boys under the age of twelve. During sentencing the judge warned him that he must change his ways or face the prospect of a long time behind bars: 'I am aware ... that you have medical problems and problems in establishing your own identity. Now, people can understand and have sympathy for that but it does not permit you to go around doing these sort of things for your own gratification,' the judge cautioned. For his part, Lane blamed his behaviour on his family, whom he said 'prevent me from living my lifestyle as I wish to live it ... If I done [sic] such a foolish thing again ... I'd rather be chucked away for life and the keys chucked away.'

But Lane had no intention of curbing his behaviour. For him, a young truant like Robert Wagner was easy prey.

*   *   *

It was not until the end of 1989, after four years in hiding, that Robert Wagner and Barry Lane reappeared as suddenly as they had vanished. Pleased to be reunited with her son, Wagner's mother would visit regularly, although Lane – who no longer dressed in drag – was never far away. Wagner told his mother that Lane had whisked him away so that authorities could not separate them. Now that he was eighteen, there was nothing they could do.

Lane and Wagner were sharing a small house in the northern Adelaide suburb of Salisbury North. The yards were unkempt and the home filthy. Anyone who visited could barely stand the putrid odour coming from inside the house, the result of their pet cats having soiled the carpets and floors.

Obviously gay, the couple was constantly harassed by bigoted locals who would spray graffiti on their front fence, eventually forcing them to invest in two large Rottweiler dogs for protection. Other neighbours were more friendly, some lending Lane money or giving him cigarettes.

Lane and Wagner would spend much of their time wandering through the neighbourhood, and one day late in 1991 they met a young couple moving into a house not far from theirs. The man introduced himself as John Bunting; his wife's name was Veronika.

With his burning hate of homosexuals and paedophiles, it's likely John Bunting initially despised both Robert Wagner and Barry Lane. However, after getting to know them a little better, he saw opportunity.

Bunting's own childhood sexual abuse caused him to feel sympathy for Wagner, who he suspected was not homosexual by choice but had been coerced by Lane, the paedophile. Bunting decided to take the young man under his wing, to rescue him.

At the same time, Bunting did not want to merely cast Lane aside — he was far too useful for that. As he developed a close bond with Wagner, Bunting feigned friendship with Lane in order to extract information from him about other paedophiles.

John Bunting had found the perfect way to feed his obsession.

About the time he befriended Wagner and Lane, Bunting had also met a man named Mark at a welding course and the pair had become mates. Mark Haydon — who had changed his surname from Lawrence — was a quiet man, almost withdrawn, but with a foul temper. He had not been blessed with a sharp intellect, or a fortunate life.

Haydon was raised almost single-handedly by his father, Edward Lawrence. His mother suffered schizophrenia and was forever checking in and out of hospital. She died in 1996. Haydon's only sibling, an older brother, had been killed in a car crash in 1972.

As a young man Haydon shared the family home with his father, and his first job was at the car manufacturing plant where Edward had been a spray painter for more than a decade. After less than two years Haydon was sacked for stealing. He worked little from then on.

Haydon had few girlfriends but in 1992 he moved in with a woman named Christina. The couple had a son, but their relationship soured within months of the birth. In 1994 he began a relationship with Verna Sinclair.

Verna — who often went by her middle name, Audrey — had endured an unsettled childhood. She was the youngest of seven children and most of her brothers and sisters had been fostered or adopted out. As a young woman Verna had led a nomadic existence, drifting around Australia. Between 1978 and 1988 she gave birth to seven children, six boys and a girl, who were fathered by five different men. Devoid of any maternal skills or instincts, Verna placed her first three children into care, dumped the next two with one of her sisters and kept only the two youngest, William and Christopher.

Not long after the relationship began, Verna and her sons moved into the house Haydon shared with his father. The following year Edward shifted into a nursing home, having suffered a fall while the others were on holiday. In 1997 Mark and Verna married and, concerned that one of her ex-partners might try to find her, the new bride changed her name to Elizabeth Audrey Haydon. In 1998 the couple sold Mark Haydon's family home and bought another, in the northern suburb of Smithfield Plains.

FOUR

While tragedy touches the lives of many, it stalked Elizabeth Harvey throughout her forty-seven years of life, striking not only at her but at those she loved.

Her birth name was Christine Anne Youde, and would change many times. One of three children to parents Dennis and Joyce Youde, Elizabeth had a miserable life almost from the day it began in September 1953. She was young when her mother left her father for a man who was an abusive drunk, taking her children with her. The children were rid of their stepfather only when he died suddenly.

Harvey grew up to be an intelligent woman but the horrors she had endured at the hands of her stepfather meant that in adulthood she suffered almost constantly from depression. From this stemmed a weakness which would destroy her life: Harvey could not be without a man.

Harvey's first child, Troy Youde, was born on 30 August 1976, but his father left her to cope with motherhood alone. Within two years Harvey had met and married another, much older, man. Spyros Vlassakis had been born in Greece and lived in Egypt, before taking a job on a cargo vessel and jumping ship in Australia.

Spyros was accepting of Troy at first, even agreeing to have his name placed on the toddler's birth certificate. On

Christmas Eve 1979, Harvey gave birth to the couple's first son, James Spyridon Vlassakis. Adrian Vlassakis was born two years later and the youngest, Kristoffer, in 1985.

The family lived in Adelaide's northern suburbs, both parents failing to hold down a regular job, preferring instead to rely on government welfare payments. They would even joke that Kristoffer had been 'born for the benefit'.

The family led a troubled life, with Harvey and Spyros often separating. In addition, there was the family's dark secret – Spyros's sustained, brutal sexual abuse of both Troy and Jamie. In a disturbingly similar story to that of their mother's abusive childhood, the brothers escaped Spyros's abuse only when he died suddenly in the winter of 1986. Spyros Vlassakis suffered a massive heart attack as he fetched Jamie a glass of water, the young boy watching as paramedics lost the battle to save his father's life.

Now a widow, Elizabeth Harvey (then named Christine Vlassakis) wasted little time in mourning. She once again yearned to have a man in her life, and while at a friend's party met her new love. His name was Marcus Johnson.

Many men would be quick to shy away from a recently widowed mother of four, but Marcus liked Harvey from the moment they met. In any case, he too had 'baggage'.

In 1971 Marcus had married a young girl named Carlyne Heitmann and together they had three sons – the first, Nigel, and twin boys David and Michael. By 1980 the marriage had crumbled and the pair divorced. Carlyne was granted sole custody of the boys and would later remarry, then move interstate. Gradually Marcus lost contact with his sons.

Marcus and Elizabeth's union was as peculiar as it was tumultuous. They were in no rush to get married, instead opting for a de facto relationship. There was a string of brief separations, brought on at least in part by Troy and

Jamie's rejection of Marcus. Troy especially resented Marcus's relationship with his mother and spent time living with his grandmother. Throughout this period the family moved house more than a dozen times, almost always at Harvey's instigation, often forcing the boys to change schools. Their academic achievement suffered as a result.

Despite the irregular lifestyle, Marcus held down a job at a local car manufacturing plant, and stood by Harvey and her boys. In 1992 the couple officially married. Wedlock did nothing to improve the stormy relationship, which deteriorated even further as depression took a hold on Harvey's life. The news that her mother was dying of cancer pushed her to the brink of a nervous breakdown and she became hopelessly addicted to shopping and gambling on poker machines. Strangely, she also became obsessed with arts and crafts, enrolling in class after class.

Ten months after deciding to marry, Elizabeth and Marcus parted. The split was amicable and Marcus continued to see the boys, who would sometimes live with him.

By October 1993 Elizabeth Harvey's mental state had deteriorated further. She was hooked on prescription drugs and neglecting her sons, spending little time at home as she cared for her ailing mother. Thankfully a seemingly kind neighbour named Jeffrey Payne was only too happy to lend a hand. He befriended the boys, won Harvey's trust, and before long took over the role of caring for the youngsters while their mother was away. What Harvey didn't know was that Payne was a paedophile.

From November 1993 – the month Harvey's mother died – until January of the following year, Payne preyed on the boys on an almost daily basis. Jamie was shown pornography and told that if he complied his younger brothers would be left alone. If he said anything to his mother, Payne warned, she would be murdered.

When Harvey finally learned of her sons' abuse, the police were called and on 3 March 1994, Jeffrey Edwin Payne was arrested. At first he denied the crimes but he confessed during his interview with police. Disturbingly, the sex offender whom a psychiatrist found had 'little willpower over offending against young children' was released on bail and allowed to return home to the street where his victims still lived. Payne would sit outside his home across the road and yell taunts at Jamie and his brothers, referring to them as 'my boys'. Payne was eventually convicted and sentenced to four years in jail. But the fact that Payne had been initially released on bail caused the young Jamie to develop a strong distrust of the police.

This horrific betrayal had a devastating effect on the boys, none more so than Jamie. The fourteen year old, like his mother, plunged into depression. He struggled at school, felt ashamed even to face his family and became obsessive about showering, sometimes scrubbing himself until he bled. Jamie also turned to drugs and alcohol, which he began to use heavily. For Harvey the abuse triggered memories of her childhood ordeal and precipitated a complete nervous breakdown. She was forced to face the terrible reality that her neglect of her children had left them vulnerable and had played into the hands of a predator.

This was a family in crisis; a mother and her children desperate for help, for someone to turn to.

Barry Lane had watched from a distance as Jeffrey Payne stalked Elizabeth Harvey's children. Jealous that he could not have the boys for himself, it was Lane who warned Harvey that Payne was preying on her sons.

Lane had also told John Bunting of the young family's plight and, fuelled by his hatred of paedophiles, Bunting decided he should be the one to protect them. It was late one afternoon when he rode to the family's home on his motorcycle, knocked on the door and introduced himself to Harvey. He explained that she should beware of Barry Lane because he too was a child molester who wanted only to get his hands on her sons.

By the end of 1994 Bunting was in a sexual relationship with Harvey, his marriage to Veronika all but over.

For James Vlassakis, this man on the motorcycle who had appeared from nowhere to save his family was a hero. After all he had endured, Jamie was desperate for a father figure and Bunting had walked into his life at just the right moment. Jamie liked – even loved – John Bunting. He saw a man who was intelligent, well spoken and polite, who possessed an air of authority and power. By the time the fourteen-year-old asked Bunting to be his father, the pair was already very close.

At first, Jamie's relationship with Bunting seemed harmless, even positive. They would take motorbike rides together and go to the movies. Bunting even encouraged Jamie to return to school. But Bunting's darker side soon emerged. Jamie began to notice Bunting's odd traits, his fixation with his gun collection and his weird habit of searching people's rooms when they weren't around.

Bunting would kill cats and dogs and encourage Jamie to watch as he skinned them. One time he played music in the background as he trapped a dog and demanded that Jamie shoot it in the head. When the young teenager baulked at pulling the trigger, Bunting did it himself.

Perhaps most disturbing was Bunting's maniacal hatred of paedophiles. Bunting would talk almost daily of violent retribution against child molesters and gays. These 'dirties', he said, didn't deserve to live. Bunting also confided in Jamie that he too had been the victim of child abuse.

A shrine to Bunting's obsession was his 'Wall of Spiders'. On a bedroom wall he would stick pieces of yellow paper, each bearing the name and personal details of a person he believed was a paedophile. He would write comments about these 'rock spiders' – they included 'prefers young boys' or 'plays Santa Claus at Christmas and has been banned by the stores'. The papers were linked together with lengths of blue string, forming a wall chart which more closely resembled a spider's web.

Bunting's suspects were also his targets. He would randomly select a person's name from the wall and then torment them. Most often it was nuisance phone calls, although sometimes Bunting would take Jamie and they would graffiti the person's house or pour brake fluid on their car.

In addition to his Wall of Spiders, Bunting kept detailed dossiers in which he meticulously recorded people's personal details, interests and what he believed was their 'type of deviance'. Most of this information was gleaned from Barry Lane – it was the very reason Bunting had befriended him. The dossier on Lane was by far the most extensive:

Interests: Hanging around toilet blocks looking for young children, wearing poofter pants that show all his wares, punching dung with anyone and everything, making a constant nuisance of himself and flaunting the great side of homosexuality if anyone is stupid enough to listen.

Type of Deviance: Rock spider, dobs in other rock spiders for the ego, denies that he is one, known toucher of children especially around the age of 12–14. Would not torture victims but psychologically changes by playing power games. He believes that it is a form of love to do this to children. He has no conscious [sic] and cannot make up his/her mind if he is straight or gay or male or female. Takes hormones to create breasts and hormones to remove hair from its body.

Now acquainted with the real John Bunting, Jamie's love for him was overtaken by fear. The teenager's mother also experienced the terror John Bunting could instil. Early in their relationship Harvey made the near-fatal mistake of assuming it was merely a casual fling. When she began seeing another man, John held a pistol to his head and made the man beg for his life.

'John rocked up at my place while Mervyn and I were in the kitchen and he came strutting in with his gun and ranting and raving,' Harvey said later in an interview with police. 'I stood in front of Mervyn and John fired the gun but there were no bullets in the gun.'

For Harvey and her sons, there was no escaping John Bunting. From late 1995 they lived as a family, the older boys drifting in and out of home. Over the next four years the family moved from one house to the next, spending most time in the rural township of Murray Bridge, just over an hour's drive east of Adelaide. It was not until 1999 that John Bunting and Elizabeth Harvey moved back to town.

FIVE

Tuesday, 16 August 1994, was a warm and sunny day – the kind that makes office workers stare out of their windows knowing that by five o'clock the best part of the day will have passed them by.

This was never a problem for Jack Finch and his brother, Ron. For their entire adult lives the brothers, aged seventy-nine and seventy-six, had worked the land. The Finch family was a well-known farming clan in the district of Lower Light, 50 kilometres north of Adelaide. The family was highly regarded by locals, who knew Jack and Ron as a colourful duo whose friendliness and warmth was matched only by their never-ending array of witty one-liners. The brothers were always happy to stop for a chat and never too busy to lend a hand, even to complete strangers.

For Jack and Ron, the absence of wind and rain on that Tuesday meant that conditions were perfect for spraying the noxious weeds which often spread over their properties. It was tough work – Jack and Ron were no strangers to that – and, worst of all, time consuming.

At 8 a.m. the brothers set off for a 4000-acre property which was home to a sizable proportion of their 2000 sheep. Leased by the family from various owners for almost sixty years, the property was about 4 kilometres west of Jack's rustic homestead and about 9 kilometres in the same direction from the small, shabby town of Lower Light. The Finch family leased the property from the federal government, which once had plans to build an airstrip there. It was a project that would never be completed, although a radio communications tower remains to this day.

The brothers worked all morning, Jack driving his beaten-up Toyota utility, a tank filled with poison on the back. Ron walked beside, armed with the weed-spraying gun. Sweat dripped from the men's brows as they laboured through ankle-high scrub, consisting mostly of saltbush and weeds. After a lunch break the pair returned to the same paddock but began spraying in a different area, not far from a dirt track running towards the radio tower. Jack was taking care to avoid getting thorns in the ute's tyres when Ron yelled at him to stop. 'There's a fox burrow there,' he said. 'And you're almost in it.'

Jack steered around the obstacle, neither of the men taking much notice. A few metres further on Ron spotted what he at first thought was a sheep bone, the sharp white colour attracting his interest. On closer inspection there was no doubt: this was a human skull.

Ron picked up the skull, cradled it in his hand and looked carefully. At the back there was a large dent. Whoever this person was, they'd been dealt a fierce blow. 'That's somebody's grave back there,' Ron said to his brother, as they returned to the ditch they had steered around moments before.

It was a shallow grave, about 10 centimetres deep. There were no clothes, just the skeletal remains, and no obvious signs of identification such as a wallet or jewellery. Whoever had dumped the body had made only a cursory attempt to bury it, and bones had since been scattered as far as 50 metres away by foxes and birds.

Not far from where the Finch brothers made the find there is a road often travelled by locals, which leads to a nearby beach. Along the way the road changes from firm graded stone to a dirt strip on which even some four-wheel drives cannot travel in the wet. Jack figured that whoever had discarded the body had most likely planned to do so at the beach, but found the road too boggy to continue. Their only other option was the Finch brothers' paddock.

Within an hour of the find a large portion of scrubland had been cordoned off and specialist crime scene police were on their way. Also travelling from the heart of Adelaide were detectives from the South Australia Police Major Crime Branch.

The discovery attracted immediate media interest and, after a cursory examination by a pathologist, police publicly confirmed they were investigating a murder.

The media speculated that the bones could those be of a twelve-year-old girl, Rhianna Barreau, who had vanished two years before from Adelaide's southern suburbs. It was one of the most notorious cases of suspected abduction and murder in the state's modern history. Her body has yet to be found.

The find also prompted a media mention of one of Australia's worst serial murders, the so-called 'Family' killings in which five young men were abducted, sexually abused, mutilated and murdered. In 1982 the body of one of the suspected victims, fourteen-year-old schoolboy Peter Stogneff, was found not far from Lower Light at a place called Middle Beach. As quickly as the media speculated on such connections, however, detectives ruled them out. The following day police, crawling on hands and knees, combed the land surrounding the shallow grave for any clues that may be lying nearby. Even at this early stage detectives knew that finding a wallet or some other clue to the victim's identity was of vital importance. It would not be that easy. Expert crime scene officers painstakingly excavated the grave, taking a series of photographs which, they believed, would one day be presented in court. In all, officers spent three days at the scene.

The most detailed operation, however, was the one performed for the next month by forensic pathologist Ross James, who pieced together much of the skeleton to develop a profile of the 'John Doe'. He was able to determine that this was a male, probably about seventeen years old. He had been savagely beaten about the head and dumped face down in the paddock, possibly as long ago as two years before his remains were discovered.

The murder victim was about 172 centimetres tall and had been slightly built. Examination of the left shoulder joint, which was more developed than the right, suggested the teenager was left-handed. He had a long jaw, a narrow nose, and at the time of his death his hair was dyed copper-blond. At some stage the man had suffered a broken collarbone and his teeth were in perfect condition – initially offering detectives hope that their victim would be quickly identified through dental records.

Not long after the remains were discovered police made a public appeal, with one of the detectives on the case remarking, 'Somebody, or a group of people, has lost a mate. He's got friends, his friends must have missed him. Someone knows something.'

Working on this theory, police began the arduous task of sifting through files on South Australia's missing persons, at the time numbering about 135. Missing persons from other parts of Australia also could not be ruled out. Was this man a backpacker? Was he a hitchhiker?

Forensic experts using facial reconstruction techniques came up with an image of a man's face they believed was similar to the victim's, but again no one came forward. The South Australian government posted a $100,000 reward, also without success.

Eventually the remains the Finch brothers had discovered in their paddock at Lower Light were placed in storage at the State Forensic Science Centre in Adelaide, and the case took a back seat to more recent murders.

One senior officer would later describe the John Doe case as one of the most frustrating he had encountered: 'It is the only case we have on our records where we have determined murder is the cause but we are unable to identify the victim. The fact that no one has come forward is mystifying. We have checked hundreds of missing persons files throughout Australia and overseas.'

What the police didn't know was why their tireless efforts to match John Doe with a name on a missing person's report had been futile: he hadn't yet been reported missing.

It was the afternoon of 26 October 1995, when the missing person's report rolled off the fax machine: *Clinton Douglas Trezise, date of birth 5/12/1973*.

The Missing Persons Section received reports like this almost every day. What made this case peculiar, though, was the length of time it had taken Clinton's family to report him missing. The young man's relatives had not seen nor heard from him since 1992. Owing to a volatile family history, they'd assumed he had chosen to leave.

Police checks revealed that their last record of Clinton

Trezise was in May 1992. Interstate searches yielded nothing. Inquiries with the state government's Family and Community Services Department showed Clinton had last sought its help in July 1992, when he attended a department office for financial counselling. That same month, on the 22nd, was the last time Clinton withdrew money from his bank account. While his disability pension continued to be paid in, the funds remained untouched.

An obvious line of inquiry for missing persons investigators was the discovery of a young man's skeleton in a paddock at Lower Light a year before. A photograph of Trezise was sent to the Forensic Science Centre, where it was compared with the Lower Light skull.

Twice an expert deemed the remains to be not those of Clinton Trezise. Sadly, the expert had made a mistake. The missing teenager and the remains were, in fact, one and the same. The error would not be detected for another four years — and after another eleven murders.

SIX

In Australia around 30,000 people are reported missing every year. Close to 5,000 of those cases are in South Australia. Some missing people engineer their own disappearances – often for domestic or financial reasons – while others, tragically, have taken their own lives.

Then there are those who have met with foul play.

In close to half of the missing persons cases investigated by the South Australian police, the subject is located within forty-eight hours. Ninety-nine per cent are found, dead or alive, within twelve months. It was the remaining one per cent that bothered Detective Superintendent Paul Schramm.

Soon after taking control of the Police Major Crime Branch, Schramm decided that the 'one per centers' needed closer scrutiny. Too often, Schramm believed, old missing persons cases were allowed to collect dust in a detective's filing cabinet while family members gave up hope. It was not good enough to assume that these people had vanished of their own free will – there was always the chance they had been murdered and that their killers remained at large.

Such attention to detail had been a trademark of Paul Schramm's career. No matter what he chose to do with his life, he would undoubtedly have excelled. It just so happened that, as a fresh-faced teenager in 1965, he had chosen to become a cop.

By twenty-two Schramm was a detective, first assigned to suburban investigation units, then to the Major Crime and Fraud branches. At thirty-three, he was promoted to the rank of commissioned officer and served as head of the Drug Squad before returning to Fraud, this time as its boss.

In 1995, now a Detective Superintendent, Paul Schramm was appointed to one of the police department's most coveted and prestigious positions – officer in charge of the Major Crime Branch.

Taking charge of Major Crime meant a high profile and intense pressure. The Major Crime boss had to not only supervise investigations into the state's most serious crimes – mostly homicides – but also cope with constant attention from superiors and demands for swift justice from victims' families. As well, there was the glare of the public spotlight and the hungry hordes of media following almost every investigation.

It was a challenge to which Paul Schramm was well suited. He possessed years of experience combined with a flair for leadership. A tall, slender man, always impeccably dressed, Schramm is highly intelligent, meticulous and a true strategist. Renowned as a national expert in the management of serious crime investigations, he has superior powers of analysis and communication. Every word that passes Paul Schramm's lips is carefully considered and delivered to great effect.

When he was first handed the missing persons file, Detective Senior Constable Craig Patterson didn't have a lot of time to look it over. Having not long ago been transferred into Major Crime, he already had several current cases to work on. However, Superintendent Schramm had decided that major crime detectives were to use their 'downtime' to re-examine cases where the trail had gone cold. This missing persons file had been assigned to Patterson and he would have to deal with it.

Patterson may have been new to major crime, but he was no rookie: he'd been in the job for eighteen years and a detective for more than a decade. It was July 1997 when he first looked over the file which bore the name Clinton Douglas Trezise.

Clinton Trezise had been reported missing by his mother in October 1995 but had apparently vanished some considerable time before. The family had not been close, which explained the amount of time elapsed between Clinton's disappearance and the report to police.

Patterson began his investigation by reviewing the inquiries already undertaken by officers in the police Missing Persons Section. At the time Trezise vanished, the eighteen-year-old had been living in a flat in the northern Adelaide suburb of Elizabeth. His television and other electrical goods vanished when he did, but Trezise had left behind other belongings, including personal papers. Later the flat was cleared out by his family.

Clinton had been on welfare benefits, having suffered an injury which prevented him from working. Checks with government agencies revealed the last contact with him was on 10 July 1992. The last withdrawal from his bank account had been twelve days later. There was no record of Clinton Trezise with other police departments around Australia, nor did the Immigration Department have any record of him leaving the country. He didn't even have a passport.

Patterson noted with interest a reference in the Trezise file to the skeletal remains of a young man which had been discovered in a paddock at Lower Light in 1994. Initially it was thought that these may have been the remains of Clinton Trezise, but a forensic expert had compared the skull with a photograph of Trezise and concluded that they were not the same person.

For another four months Patterson made no progress in his search for Clinton Trezise. It was a low-priority case and he was able to devote only small periods of time to it. The first breakthrough came in November 1997, when the Missing Persons Section informed Patterson of yet another disappearance. A man named Barry Lane had also vanished. He had known Clinton Trezise.

Joanna Smith* met Barry Lane through the Salvation Army. Together they would attend services and church outings. Soon after the couple first met, Lane, forty-two, confessed that he was homosexual and had once been a transvestite. He explained that he had since been 'cleansed'.

Lane and Joanna enjoyed each other's company, and within two months the couple was engaged, although they continued to live apart. It was a step Joanna would never have taken had she known Barry Lane was a convicted paedophile. Her suspicions about Lane were aroused only when child welfare authorities stepped in to ensure he was never alone with Joanna's three young children.

From that point on, Lane and Joanna's relationship deteriorated. The final straw came on 26 April 1997, when Lane allowed a young man named Thomas Trevilyan to move in with him. It was Thomas's eighteenth birthday.

As far as Joanna was concerned, this teenager named Thomas was nothing but trouble. Her opinion seemed justified when Lane complained to her about Thomas's violent nature, in particular an incident when the young man had slashed him with a knife.

Despite their split, Joanna kept in contact with Lane. The last she heard from him was a telephone call in

October 1997. He and Thomas had been stranded in a country town north of Adelaide. Their car, Lane explained, had broken down and they wanted her to check the mail and feed their dogs.

A few days passed and Joanna became worried – a neighbour told her only Thomas had returned. A week later there was still no sign of anyone at Lane's house. After waiting a couple more days Joanna again spoke to the neighbour, who revealed that Thomas's grandmother had called in to collect his belongings. The teenager had killed himself.

Confused and worried about the strange series of events, Joanna went to the police to report Lane missing. Not only did she tell them that Thomas had committed suicide, but she related a story which Lane had told her only a few months before he vanished.

Barry had confessed to Joanna that he had once helped Robert Wagner dispose of human remains which had been wrapped in garbage bags and dumped somewhere 'up north'. Lane believed that the remains were those of Clinton Trezise.

The mention of Clinton Trezise in the Lane case triggered alarm bells within the police department. Detective Patterson, still assigned to the Trezise investigation, was told immediately. He asked to be informed the minute Barry Lane was located.

For seven months officers in the Missing Persons Section conducted routine inquiries to trace Barry Lane, but to no avail. The investigation intensified after a phone call from his sister, Krystal. She said her family had heard nothing of Lane since the time he was reported missing and she feared for his safety. Krystal explained that her brother was homosexual, a cross-dresser and a paedophile.

Constable Janet Forrest decided it was wise to have another look at Lane's disappearance and, using police records, managed to locate a former neighbour of Lane's. The man said he hadn't seen Lane for more than a year, but he knew someone who had: John Bunting.

John Bunting, also a former neighbour of Lane's, had been telling friends he'd seen Barry Lane in the town of Murray Bridge, east of Adelaide. Bunting now lived in the town with his partner, Elizabeth Harvey. When Constable Forrest telephoned to follow up the lead, it was Harvey who took the call.

An agitated Harvey told Forrest that Lane was a paedophile and couldn't be trusted. She said her partner, Bunting, had seen Lane three weeks before, but they didn't know where he was living. The best person to ask, Harvey suggested, was Robert Wagner. After all, Wagner and Lane had lived together for many years.

Wagner was little help. He told Constable Forrest that, by choice, he had no contact with Lane and had not spoken to him for some time. But Wagner claimed to have seen Lane at a local shopping centre 'a couple of weeks ago'. It was not the last time police would encounter Robert Wagner. Soon he would become the focus of their investigation.

The series of facts created a sinister picture:

- Clinton Trezise – vanished in 1992.
- Barry Lane – vanished October 1997.
- Lane had been an associate of Trezise.
- Lane had confessed to involvement in Trezise's disappearance.
- Soon after Lane vanished, his teenage lover Thomas Trevilyan was found dead. Apparently suicide by hanging.

Above: (left to right) Robert Wagner, John Bunting and Mark Haydon are
ed into court on the day of their arrests, 21 May 1999.

© *The Advertiser*, by Michael Milnes

Below: Robert Wagner gesticulates to the camera as he is taken with
Mark Haydon (left) and John Bunting (second left) into the Adelaide
Magistrates Court for their committal hearing.

© *The Advertiser*, by Campbell Brodie

Above: John Bunting sitting at the table of his home at 203 Waterloo Corner Road, Salisbury North. Two of his victims were buried in the back yard.

Right: John Bunting at the motor museum, where he worked in 1988.

THE MOST RECENT DONATION TO THE NATIONAL MOTOR MUSEUM

...unting in custody in 1999.

© *The Advertiser*, by Campbell Brodie

Left: A young Robert Wagner poses with his puppy. He named one of his dogs Adolf, after Hitler.

Below: Wagner peers out of a prison van.

© Photograph by Dean Faulkner

Left: Mark Haydon in custody.
© *The Advertiser*, by Campbell Brodie

Right: James Vlassakis in custody. His face is obscured due to legal restrictions in South Australia.
© *The Advertiser*, by Campbell Brodie

Above: The Snowtown house where the killers had stored Mark Haydon's four-wheel drive, with the bodies in the barrels inside.

Below: The home shared by Mark and Elizabeth Haydon, where she was murdered and bodies were stored in the garage.

Above: A police guard outside the former Bank SA building in Snowtown in the days after the bodies were found in the bank's vault (*below*).

Above: Paul Schramm speaking at the 1999 press conference announcing that bodies had been found in Snowtown.

© *Newspix*, by Matt Turne

Below: Robert Wagner, in handcuffs, being led through the streets of Snowtown as part of a jury viewing during his and Bunting's trial.

© *Newspix*, Chris Crer

Detective Patterson viewed this picture with great suspicion. He wasted little time arranging a meeting with the suburban detectives investigating the Lane and Trevilyan cases. He would review these cases too – perhaps something in the files would provide a lead. Something did: a statement given by a woman named Lenore Penner.

Lenore Penner was Thomas Trevilyan's cousin. They were related only by marriage, but Lenore had a soft spot for Thomas, whom she knew to be a deeply troubled teenager. He was mentally ill and would drift in and out of reality. Thomas dressed in army clothing and outwardly lived a fantasy in which he had served in the armed forces. Sometimes he was a sergeant, other times a major, even a lieutenant.

Lenore had learned to listen to her cousin Tommy but believe little of what he said. After his death, however, she feared one of his tales might have been true. It was a story she recorded in her diary the very day Thomas had told it to her – 30 October 1997:

Tommy came over tonight. He swore me to secrecy. He told me that he and two other friends killed Barry Lane because Barry had abused them.

They wrapped him in tape and in a garbage bag and left him there for four days.

Then they came back and put his body in the trunk of the car – killed his dogs and cats and put their guts in the trunk as well.

Then they drove somewhere and put Barry's body in a 40-gallon drum and left it. Now they have to dispose of the drum.

He's thinking either to dig a hole and bury the drum or get a speedboat and drop it in the ocean.

I don't believe him because none of these 'crisis' stories
he tells me ever seem to be his own experience.

Lenore knew Thomas had been living with a man named
Barry and, after learning of Thomas's death only a month
after he'd told her the story, immediately went to the police.
She recounted the story in even greater detail: 'Thomas said
that they tortured Barry so that he would tell them his
social security numbers, then they would withdraw the
money and divide it between them. The reason they did this
was so the police wouldn't find what they had done to
Barry and that everything would seem as normal.' Thomas
also told his cousin that he feared the other two killers were
now 'after him'. Four days later, Thomas was dead.

After initially passing on this bizarre tale of murder,
Lenore was told by one detective not to worry. Barry Lane,
the police believed, was in Queensland.

However, by the time he visited Lenore Penner,
Detective Patterson was not so sure. It was time to step up
the investigation.

The suggestion that Barry Lane's bank account was being
pilfered by the men who'd killed him established an
obvious line of inquiry for Detective Patterson. Checks
with the government's Social Security Department
confirmed that Lane received a fortnightly pension of
$353.20. The cash was paid directly into an account he held
with Bank SA.

Patterson then discovered a disturbing pattern in Lane's
bank records. Prior to Lane's disappearance in October
1997, he would withdraw his pension from automatic teller
machines (ATMs) near his home. Immediately after the
date Lane was reported missing, the withdrawals began to

occur from outlets some distance away. Most were from an ATM at the BP Express service station in the northern Adelaide suburb of Elizabeth Vale.

Either Barry Lane had moved – without telling his family and friends – or his bankcard had moved without him. Detective Patterson figured there was one easy way to find out.

The camera was hidden. Only staff at the BP Express knew it was there and they'd been asked to keep quiet. Police had installed the camera saying it was part of an ongoing investigation and management was assured it had nothing to do with any employees. The police technicians had come on 1 July 1998 and exactly a week later the trap was sprung.

Oblivious to the watchful lens of the law, the tall red-haired man stood at the ATM and inserted the card at precisely 6.21 a.m. The card number was 5602 6500 0704 0960. It belonged to Barry Lane.

The man punched in a personal identification number that only Lane should have known, then hit a single key to select 'account balance'. The printed receipt showed $367.95. The man then pushed the receipt into the disposal slot and pressed a key for 'another transaction' at 6.22 a.m. Withdrawal. $360. The receipt again went into the rubbish.

Four days later, perched in front of a television screen in the Major Crime offices, Detective Patterson replayed the tape. There were only a few minutes of vision but the camera had yielded exactly what he'd hoped for: a suspect. The ATM receipts were later recovered for fingerprinting and still photographs were extracted from the video. Within a few days a northern suburbs patrol cop, one of many who'd been asked to look at the pictures, identified the man using the ATM as Robert Joe Wagner.

Investigations by the Missing Persons Section had previously established Robert Wagner as an associate of Barry Lane's. Now he'd been caught taking money from Lane's account.

A fortnight later police set another trap – this time they used a full-scale surveillance operation. From the early hours of the morning on Wednesday, 22 July, undercover police were watching Robert Wagner. They trailed him as, just before 5.30 a.m., he drove his brown Ford station wagon to the BP Express service station and withdrew another $360 from Barry Lane's account.

Later that day Wagner was followed to the town of Murray Bridge, where he visited a friend named John Bunting, also flagged in police records as an associate of Lane.

Over the next few months, surveillance was infrequent. There was no direct evidence of murder, so the case took a back seat to current homicide investigations. Despite Detective Patterson's requests, surveillance teams were continually assigned to other cases. There simply weren't enough people to go round.

In October 1998 Patterson applied to intercept Wagner and Bunting's home telephones, but resources were again a problem. There were only six intercept lines available and none could be spared.

SEVEN

John Justin BUNTING
Robert Joe WAGNER

In a perfect world, alarm bells would have been ringing. Someone would have noticed sooner or a computer database would have alerted police.

John Justin BUNTING
Robert Joe WAGNER

The two names had come to the attention of detectives investigating the disappearance of Clinton Trezise and Barry Lane. They were suspects.

John Justin BUNTING
Robert Joe WAGNER

However, the detectives weren't aware of a sinister coincidence. The two names also featured in another missing persons case: Suzanne Allen, whom Bunting and Wagner both knew, had vanished in 1996.

Suzanne Allen's family and friends remember her as a warm, friendly woman. Sadly, she drifted through life hoping for something better, only to meet with a horrific end.

Suzanne was 'a little slow', according to friends, and more than a little vulnerable. Easily led and, ultimately, easy prey.

Born on 26 June 1949, Suzan (later changed to Suzanne) Phyllis Martin was one of seven children raised in the Victorian town of Mildura. She moved out of the family home at fourteen and crossed the border into New South Wales, where she worked on a sheep station.

In 1983, with two failed marriages and four children behind her, Suzanne decided to seek out a new life.

She travelled to South Australia, settling in Adelaide's northern suburbs. Her children remained with their fathers and Suzanne had little contact with them, visiting once or twice a year and sending cards for birthdays and Christmas.

Suzanne's 'new' life consisted of one failed relationship after another. She would meet men at singles' clubs, throw herself into love, then come crashing out.

In 1993 Suzanne's live-in lover was a young man named Ray Davies. At one point the couple was engaged, although Ray was sleeping on the lounge at the time. Davies had a slight intellectual handicap, was unemployed and nineteen years Suzanne's junior. The pair passed the time collecting cans and bottles, using the extra cash to boost their government welfare pensions. When their relationship floundered, Suzanne allowed Ray to live in a caravan in her back yard.

It may have been Suzanne Allen's unique lifestyle or bizarre friends like Ray Davies. Perhaps it was the fact that her mostly jobless neighbours had nothing better to do.

Whatever the reason, Suzanne Allen became a local spectacle from almost the moment she moved into 3 Ghent Street, Salisbury North.

One neighbour, Marilyn Nelson, would later detail for police the strange goings-on at Suzanne Allen's house:

Whilst she lived there, she had a few really odd blokes visit her. She used to pick them up from the karaoke club . . .

They were all mentally retarded, they weren't normal people as such, they all had some form of mental problems. Suzanne too had some form of mental problems, she was a bit backward.

I know that she did have a young guy stay with her for some time, his name was Ray. He was in his mid-twenties, he was mentally retarded, the neighbours were scared of this person because he would hide in the bushes and when the young girls would walk past he would play with himself. He would expose himself to the young girls, there was a complaint made to the police about him. We eventually told Suzanne and she kicked him out.

Suzanne used to keep to herself. She was friendly with all the neighbours.

Marilyn Nelson was among the first people to notice that Suzanne had disappeared. At first she thought nothing of it – after all, Suzanne had talked about moving.

It was a visit from Suzanne's brother, John Martin, which got Marilyn thinking all might not be well. John explained that his sister had vanished, leaving behind her pets and most of her possessions. Only her car was gone.

Marilyn agreed to keep a lookout. Six days later, on 3 December 1996, the watchful neighbour noticed a truck parked in Suzanne's driveway and confronted one of the strangers inside the house:

I asked him if I could speak to her brother John. He said he didn't know anybody by that name and that is when I became suspicious, so I went to the phone box and rang the police.

Police received the call at 2.18 p.m. Sixteen minutes later a patrol was on scene. As the police officers approached the house, two men were carrying furniture to a truck. The men claimed they were friends of Suzanne's and were helping her move, the shorter, rotund fellow producing a key to the front door which he said Suzanne had given him.

While the policemen had no reason to doubt the men's story, one of the officers asked for their details and wrote them in his notebook:

John Justin BUNTING
30 years, dob 4/9/66
Robert Joe WAGNER
25 years, dob 28/11/71

Suzanne Allen's brother decided it was time to report her missing on 10 December 1996. Computer checks revealed that the last known police record of her was in January of that year, when she had been charged with assault.

Suzanne's co-accused were listed as John Justin Bunting and Robert Joe Wagner. The charges were later dropped.

Missing persons investigators tried unsuccessfully to contact Bunting and Wagner, to see if they knew where Suzanne was.

In February 1997 police inquiries revealed a bank account in Suzanne's name. Regular withdrawals were occurring in the town of Murray Bridge, east of Adelaide. The mailing address for the account was also at Murray Bridge – a house occupied by John Bunting. When contacted, Bunting told police Suzanne was involved in an ongoing family feud and wanted nothing to do with her brother or anyone else.

Within months of the missing persons report being

lodged, police lost contact with Suzanne's brother. He had apparently moved on without leaving new contact details. Unable to get in touch with him – and with a seemingly credible account of Suzanne Allen's movements – the case was closed.

Just over a year later, in April 1998, police reactivated their search for Suzanne Allen. Her sister, Joan Potts, had written to the Victorian Police Commissioner asking for help, and missing persons investigators in both that state and South Australia agreed to take another look.

Once again the suggestion of a family feud seemed credible. Regular withdrawals were still being made from Suzanne's bank account – still from Murray Bridge – and the car she had previously owned was now in the possession of a friend who said she'd recently spoken to Suzanne. The 'friend' was Elizabeth Harvey – John Bunting's partner.

Having taken over the family's search for Suzanne after the death of their brother, Joan Potts was assured by police that her sister was alive and well. Perhaps, they suggested, Suzanne did not want to be found.

Joan was not so sure.

EIGHT

It was late at night and Mark Haydon resented being there. As he sat in the ground floor interview room at the Elizabeth police station in Adelaide's north, Haydon reckoned he'd made a mistake in agreeing to come in. After all, he wasn't under arrest.

An hour before, two detectives had visited Haydon's house in the working-class northern suburb of Smithfield Plains and asked him to come to the police station. The detectives explained they were investigating the disappearance of his wife, Elizabeth Audrey Haydon.

Elizabeth's sister, Gail Sinclair, also went to the station to be interviewed. She lived in a garage at the back of Mark and Elizabeth's home. Some days the house seemed very crowded – also living there were Elizabeth's two sons from a previous relationship, William and Christopher, and Gail's teenage son, Fred.

In addition, Gail's boyfriend, John Bunting, would often stay over. He was mates with Mark Haydon and the pair would spend a lot of time with another friend, Robert Wagner.

Detective Greg Stone handed Mark Haydon a writing pad and pen, asking him to outline the events immediately before and after his wife's disappearance. He told him to start by writing his full name, the time and date.

Mark Ray Haydon 11.17 p.m.   *26th November 1998*

Perhaps it was because he struggled with reading and writing, but Haydon took more than an hour and a half to write just over two pages:

Approximately one week before my wife's disappearance, I told her I was not happy with the way our house had been let become so untidy. I then went outside to work on my car ... she vented her anger on her sister Gail, then went outside in tears. The day after this she commenced cleaning the house. I did not notice any tension between my wife and her sister apart from this one incident. Our marrage [sic] was reasonably happy up until her leaving me. Sometime she would go out in the morning and not return until mid afternoon without explination [sic].

The day of our marrage [sic] breakup [this was the day Elizabeth vanished] I got up approx 9.00 a.m. My wife was already up and sitting in the lounge room having a drink of Coke. I think my sister-in-law and John Bunting were in the lounge room also. I had a drink and took my medication in the lounge room, and watched TV for a while.

At around 11.00 a.m. I put my car behind the gates and changed the starter motor. Then about 12.30 p.m. I moved the car back into the driveway. I then washed my hands and went and layed [sic] down as I had been ill most of the previous week. About 3.00 p.m. I got up and started to install a dead bolt in the back door. My friend Robert Wagner had arrived while I was asleep and helped me for a while. At about 4.30 p.m. my wife came into the kitchen and started the evening meal. Approx 4.45 my sister-in-law asked me to take her to Reynella [in Adelaide's southern suburbs] to meet someone about a dog, we left about 5.00 p.m. arriving about 7.00 p.m. We waited till about 8.30 then left to go home as no one had arrived there at the Reynella McDonald's.

On the way home I stopped at the telephones at the Bolivar Caravan Park to let my wife know we were on our way home. I could not get through so I stopped again at the phones outside the Salisbury Library. I tried to ring again and my friend John Bunting answered telling me that my wife was ranting and locked herself in our room. Gail and myself arrived home about 10.30 p.m. My friend [Bunting] then told me she [Elizabeth] had made a pass at him and she got upset when he refused her offer. I then went into her bedroom to speak to her and she accused me of sleeping with her sister Gail. I then denied the accusation and reminded her that we had never had the opportunity, and that I would not have done anything if I had. She then continued to accuse me and also called me lazy and good for nothing, I then left the room. My friend John and Gail then went out to get something to eat leaving me and my other friend Robert in the lounge room. While they were gone my wife came out of the bedroom and again accused me of being unfaithful and called me a lazy good for nothing son of a bitch, she then said she was leaving me and would ring her boyfriend [to] pick her up down the road somewhere.

At about 2.00 a.m. I went to bed and approximately 4.00 a.m. [Elizabeth] returned home drunk, got into bed and passed out. I got up about 10.30, left my wife in bed alone. My friend John and Gail came in from Gails [sic] room about 11.00 a.m. and I told them she had returned. They went out to leave us alone to sort it out. My wife got up about 11.30 a.m. I asked her where she had been, who she had been with, all she would tell me was with someone

I did not know. I asked her why she had done this and she accused me about sleeping with Gail again. She then said she was going out again, I told her to really think properly about what she was doing. She then told me I may as well go an [sic] visit my father at the nursing home and said she would wait until I returned but was gone when I got back about 4.00 p.m. as I also took a drive along the beach to think. I have not seen her since that day.

MR Haydon.

Garion Sinclair had always been worried by Mark Haydon's darker side. Garion's sister, Elizabeth Haydon, had married Mark in 1997, changing her name from Verna Sinclair.

While the couple's relationship seemed a happy one, it was not so for Elizabeth's two children who lived with the couple. Mark Haydon would often swear at William and Christopher and slap them across the face, and the boys would often be forced to squat under a table or stay in their bedrooms as punishment for even minor wrongdoings. Haydon seemed to resent the boys and Garion wondered if they would be better off elsewhere, like the rest of Elizabeth's children.

The last time Garion Sinclair saw Elizabeth was on the night of Friday, 20 November 1998. She and Haydon had dropped the boys at his house to spend the weekend. The children were to be picked up on Sunday.

Sunday morning came and Garion received a telephone call from another of his sisters. She said Mark Haydon had called to tell her Elizabeth had 'taken off'. That evening Haydon turned up at Garion's house to collect the boys, but told a different story about Elizabeth's whereabouts: he said she was home sleeping.

The next day William and Christopher arrived back at Garion's house, having walked almost two hours to get there: they told their uncle that Elizabeth was missing. When Garion confronted Haydon, his brother-in-law told him Elizabeth had come home drunk early Sunday morning then run off with a 'boyfriend' a few hours later. Haydon claimed Elizabeth had cleaned out his bank account, as well as his elderly father's, before leaving.

Garion Sinclair didn't believe Mark Haydon's story. Elizabeth had spent almost all of her time with Haydon, so it was difficult to imagine she'd had the opportunity to meet another man. Garion also didn't believe she would leave William and Christopher behind. Elizabeth had been a poor mother in the past, but appeared to be getting her life together.

On Wednesday, 25 November, Garion attended the Elizabeth police station to report his sister missing.

Elizabeth Audrey Haydon. Date of birth 29 August 1961.

Detective Senior Constable Greg Stone skimmed the missing persons file he had just been handed. It was the evening of 26 November and Stone was just starting a nightshift. The detective had been told this case was a priority because of fears for the woman's safety.

Stone was an inexperienced detective, but an intelligent, insightful man and a good cop. He began by making a few notes:

Elizabeth Haydon — m/p. Mark Haydon — husband.
4 Blackham Cr Smithfield Plains . . .
    Garion Sinclair — brother.

Stone then telephoned Garion Sinclair, adding more information to his case notes:

> Claims Mark told him on Monday 23/11 that Elizabeth has taken a lot of money from his and his father's bank account. Elizabeth's children told Gary on Monday that they did not see Elizabeth on the Sunday when they went home.
>
> Gary's worst fears are that Mark has murdered Elizabeth.

An hour later Detective Stone and another officer visited Blackham Crescent and asked Mark Haydon and Gail Sinclair to come down to the station. In his own writing, Haydon detailed the events before and after his wife's disappearance. Gail told a similar story – her statement was recorded in a separate interview room.

Both Haydon and Gail had mentioned John Bunting. He too had been present on the day Elizabeth vanished, and Detective Stone decided he should be spoken to. Bunting was living in the town of Murray Bridge, east of Adelaide, so Stone had a local patrol call by and arrangements were made for him to meet with police and give a statement.

Four days later John Bunting turned up at the Elizabeth police station to give his version of the events surrounding Elizabeth Haydon's disappearance. With him was Robert Wagner, who had also been at the Haydons' home in the hours before Elizabeth vanished. Both gave similar stories to Mark Haydon's: Elizabeth had made a pass at Bunting, the couple had argued and Elizabeth had run off with another man.

Bunting wrote his statement by hand. Wagner, who could barely read and write, gave a brief statement to a policeman before rushing off. He said he had somewhere else to be.

After dealing with Bunting and Wagner, Detective Stone received a message to call a relative of Elizabeth Haydon. The caller was concerned about Elizabeth's welfare and suggested evidence could be found in the Haydons' house, prompting another visit by Detective Stone, this time with an accompanying officer. When the police arrived, only Gail Sinclair was home.

'Despite her objections, the house was searched in her presence. During the search I located four firearms in the walk-in robe of the master bedroom ... those firearms were seized,' Detective Stone would later tell the court.

'Whilst I was in the walk-in robe I located ... a black folding purse which contained documents and cards relative to Elizabeth Haydon.'

The discovery of the purse alarmed Detective Stone – if Elizabeth had left of her own free will, why would she leave her purse behind?

The following day the detectives again visited the Haydons' house, this time to search a garage in the back yard. The day before it had been locked and they hadn't been able to get in. In the centre of the garage floor was a pit cluttered with car parts and clothes. Emanating from the pit was what Stone would later describe as a 'peculiar odour'. He also noticed what he thought were insect casings on the floor.

As the investigation intensified, there would be more searches of Mark Haydon's home. Some involved specialist crime scene officers. Haydon, by now, was well aware that he was under suspicion. He didn't like the attention – nor did Bunting and Wagner. They resented this pushy detective named Stone and they knew it was a risk to have him snooping around.

NINE

It was nothing more than a routine check. Missing Persons investigator Janet Forrest tapped into the police computer as she had done countless times before. This day, 27 November 1998, she was checking on the progress of a case being handled by detectives at Elizabeth CIB, in Adelaide's north. They were tracking a missing woman named Elizabeth Haydon.

As she scrolled through the notes in the detectives' computerised journal, Constable Forrest could see the investigation was well under way:

Missing Person Elizabeth Haydon. Address 4 Blackham Cres, Smithfield Plains.

Husband Mark Haydon.

Sister Gail Sinclair. Address also 4 Blackham Cres, Smithfield Plains.

Sinclair's boyfriend, John Bunting . . .

The name caught Constable Forrest's eye. John Bunting had come to the attention of Major Crime Branch detectives investigating the disappearance of Clinton Trezise and Barry Lane. It was a secret investigation, but one which she was privy to.

John Bunting ...

The name also featured prominently in another missing persons file. The Suzanne Allen case had been reinvestigated only recently – Bunting had provided the seemingly credible explanation of Allen's whereabouts.

All of a sudden, it didn't seem so credible.

There was a flurry of activity in the Major Crime office from the moment the missing persons cases were linked. Priorities changed.

Suspicion of foul play had surrounded the Clinton Trezise and Barry Lane disappearances, but there was no evidence of murder. A man named Robert Wagner had been filmed taking cash from Lane's bank account, but that was evidence only of theft – fraud at best. Wagner and his friend, John Bunting, had been the targets of limited police surveillance operations which had yielded little more.

Detective Craig Patterson, with the help of his partner, Brian Swan, had been working the case whenever time permitted. Whenever resources permitted.

The discovery made by the observant missing persons investigator changed everything. Bunting and Wagner were now tied to three different cases. Three missing people.

The most recent disappearance was Elizabeth Haydon's. The prime suspect – her husband, Mark – was best of mates with John Bunting and Robert Wagner.

Detective Patterson met with the suburban detectives assigned to the Elizabeth Haydon case, but didn't reveal all. He warned his colleagues to take the matter seriously, to consider murder the most likely scenario. Patterson told them he was investigating other matters in which Bunting and Wagner were persons of interest.

The suburban detectives were told to continue the Elizabeth Haydon investigation without alerting the suspects to the parallel inquiries. Regular reports were to be sent to Major Crime.

For Detective Craig Patterson, it had all begun fifteen months ago with a seemingly straightforward case review. Then, on 6 February 1999, the disappearances of Clinton Douglas Trezise, Barry Wayne Lane, Suzanne Phyllis Allen and Elizabeth Audrey Haydon were officially declared Major Crimes.

The declaration meant that Patterson would finally be given the resources he needed. Applications were made for telephone intercepts; Wagner and Bunting's home and mobile telephones were tapped, designated operators listening 'live' to each call. Relevant call recordings were then passed to Major Crime, where detectives would review them. Most often it was Patterson who would listen.

Specialised police surveillance teams began 'working' the suspects more frequently.

Police revisited the service station where Robert Wagner had been withdrawing cash from Barry Lane's account. A new camera had been installed and Wagner was filmed making withdrawals on seven separate occasions. Each time he emptied the Lane account of the welfare payment, which had just been paid in.

Major Crime detectives had also been looking more closely at the disappearance of Suzanne Allen. Like Barry Lane, a government pension was being paid directly into her bank account. Centrelink, the government agency that pays pensions and unemployment benefits, told police that Suzanne Allen's correspondence was mailed to a post office box. Her residential address was recorded as 75 Barker Crescent, Smithfield Plains.

Police quickly discovered that the address didn't exist.

Checks with the Australian Central Credit Union revealed regular withdrawals from Suzanne Allen's bank account, the most recent from an ATM in Murray Bridge – the town where John Bunting lived.

In February 1999 Bunting moved from Murray Bridge to the northern Adelaide suburb of Craigmore. The very next withdrawal from Suzanne Allen's account was made in the nearby suburb of Munno Para.

A security camera recorded the image of the man using the service station's ATM. It was John Bunting. He was filmed again eight days later.

By April detectives were considering the possibility of a fifth victim. Suzanne Allen's former lover, Ray Davies, had apparently vanished in late 1995. At the time he'd been living in a caravan in Suzanne's back yard. Neither family nor friends had heard from him since.

Trouble was, he too was still being paid a government pension. In keeping with the pattern, regular withdrawals were being made from his account.

Police obtained security vision from the Australian Central Credit Union branches where the six most recent transactions on the Ray Davies account had occurred. The first two were at Murray Bridge, the others in Adelaide's northeastern suburbs.

These transactions had been over the counter. On each occasion the same man had posed as Ray Davies.

Again, it was John Bunting.

John Bunting believed he would never be caught. As is typical of serial killers, he thought himself smarter than the police. After all, he'd gotten away with murder – more than once.

The truth was, Bunting had been lucky, and his luck was running out.

Ironically, it was Bunting and his right-hand man, Robert Wagner, who led police to the breakthrough they'd been hoping for. Literally.

Late in the morning of Sunday, 16 May 1999, Craig Patterson and Brian Swan headed north out of Adelaide. With them was field intelligence officer Vicki Ramm. The detectives had been monitoring calls made by Bunting and Wagner on their mobile phones and come up with a lead. Call charge records revealed that the suspects had placed calls to addresses at two country towns north of Adelaide – Snowtown and Moonta. Patterson and Swan were going to check those addresses; the first stop was Snowtown.

About halfway along the highway Patterson received a call from the police surveillance team assigned to watch the suspects. They too were on the highway – and not far behind.

The major crime officers parked their car out of sight, then waited. At 12.20 p.m. they spotted Robert Wagner's brown Ford station wagon travelling along the highway towards them. As it drew closer, the detectives could see Wagner was driving, Bunting in the passenger seat. Several police surveillance cars trailed behind as the suspects sped past.

Wagner and Bunting were still being tagged as they cruised into Snowtown. At 1.07 p.m. they parked outside their friend Simon Jones's house on Railway Terrace and went inside. A short time later the pair walked towards the centre of town, undercover officers losing sight of them. A few minutes later they returned to Wagner's car and drove away. They'd been in town for less than an hour.

Patterson, Swan and Ramm waited until the suspects had left before making their way to Snowtown. Being there at the same time as Bunting and Wagner was far too risky. The Major Crime officers parked not far from 25 Railway Terrace West — the address listed on the mobile phone records, which they had come to check. It was the same house Bunting and Wagner had just visited.

Patterson and Swan stayed in the car while Ramm walked cautiously past the house, to check if there was anything of interest.

There was. In the driveway was a two-tone Toyota Land Cruiser.

The distinctive four-wheel drive had come to the attention of police months earlier. The broken-down Toyota had once been a permanent fixture outside Mark Haydon's house. About the time Elizabeth Haydon vanished, a neighbour had seen the vehicle being packed with garbage bags. The next day, it was gone.

Simon Jones was petrified. He had not been blessed with a sharp intellect, but he knew something serious was happening. And it seemed to be happening to him.

It was lunchtime when the police knocked on his door. He was home alone; his wife was in hospital and their kids at school.

The shorter detective, Steve McCoy, told Jones that police were looking for a missing woman named Elizabeth Haydon. They were interested in the old Toyota Land Cruiser in his driveway.

Jones explained that his friends John Bunting and Robert Wagner had towed the vehicle to Snowtown. Inside the Land Cruiser had been several large black drums. Their foul odour had been so powerful that they'd been moved across the road, to the old bank.

As he waited in the small room at the Snowtown police

station a few hours later, Simon Jones lamented ever having laid eyes on the four-wheel drive. He had directed the detectives to the old bank, and whatever they found there had created quite a stir. More police were arriving all the time.

TEN

By early evening on 20 May 1999 more than a dozen police, mostly detectives and crime scene officers, had assembled in Snowtown. They met at the local police station, their cars parked at the side of the building so as not to attract attention. The night's activities would have to be as discreet as possible – the last thing police needed was to be hindered by curious onlookers or, worse, hounded by the media. There was also the risk that the suspects would get wind of the find and set about destroying evidence. It was, however, less likely that they would be able to flee – covert surveillance teams had already swung into place.

Inside the police station the officer in charge of the Major Crime Branch, Detective Superintendent Paul Schramm, briefed his team. They discussed a cover story to fend off curious locals – a drug bust seemed the best scenario.

As nightfall approached the police made their way to the bank, walking in small groups to avoid suspicion. They congregated in the yard at the side of the bank, behind a tall fence, and gathered around the small LCD screen on a police digital camera to watch a replay of the horrific discovery.

This time entry to the old bank building was gained solely by crime scene examiners, dressed in overalls and wearing gloves. They cleared a designated path into the building and began scouring for clues. Senior Constable Gordon Drage recorded every step on video, first as he walked through the kitchen and toilet area, then the main part of the building. He filmed the junk stacked on top of the customer counter and on the floor nearby; there were old televisions, video recorders, computer parts and boxes. In cupboards under the counter he found garbage bags, rope, an empty soft drink bottle and a half-eaten packet of chips, plus a Stanley knife and two electric cables. Both cables had been tampered with and one was fitted with alligator clips.

Inside the vault, officers labelled the large black drums with the letters A through to F. It was 10.10 p.m. when the go-ahead was given to open the first of the barrels. The presence of acid had prompted concerns the contents of the barrels could be toxic, so Senior Constable Drage wore breathing apparatus as he made his approach. He carefully removed the plastic screw top lids of barrels A and B, then prised out the internal caps underneath.

Inside both human remains were visible, partly submerged in a murky liquid. As he filmed the contents Drage could see items of clothing and discarded rubber gloves.

Gradually the other barrels were opened to reveal similarly gruesome contents. From inside barrel E, human hands were protruding as though they were reaching out. At the top of barrel F were feet which had been cut off at the ankle.

The operation at the bank had been as low-key as possible, but still attracted the attention of some locals. One of them was sitting across the road on the balcony of the local pub.

About half past eleven, quarter to twelve, the police backed the trailer into the gutter. It was an unmarked four-wheel drive with a trailer attached.

I could smell something, it smelled like chemicals, you know.

It was about quarter past twelve when they started shifting the barrels out. The police were wearing overalls; they were bringing the barrels out on a sack truck.

One guy stayed on the trailer the whole time; the rest kept going back and forth.

The barrels looked pretty heavy, it took three or four people to lift them onto the trailer. The last one I reckon there was five.

By one o'clock in the morning on Friday, 21 May 1999, the last of the six barrels had been loaded. Their destination: the State Forensic Science Centre in Adelaide.

Almost fourteen hours had passed since police arrived at Snowtown. They had gone there investigating the disappearance of five people, looking for answers. Now they were left with many more questions. The most pressing was: how many bodies did the barrels contain? One thing was for certain – it was more than five. That meant more victims.

Dr John Gilbert cast his eyes from one barrel to the next. There were six of them, still on the trailer. As he stood in the State Forensic Science Centre's vehicle compound, he was already planning one of the most gruesome tasks he would ever have to perform.

Suggestions of acid in the barrels meant pH testing would have to be done first, for safety's sake. A chemist was called in; the pH in five of the barrels was neutral, in the other it was weakly acidic.

At precisely 1.20 p.m., Dr Gilbert, three technicians and the mortuary manager began their delicate operation. Their job was to recover the barrels' contents and preserve any evidence. It was slow and painstaking work.

Each barrel was weighed before being opened and tipped slowly onto its side. Fluid from each was decanted into a corresponding 44-gallon drum. The fire brigade had supplied the drums, which were lined with plastic. While large solid matter sank to the bottom of the barrels, smaller pieces had to be caught in a sieve, then placed in buckets, also labelled A through to F.

At 4.40 p.m., the recovery of body parts and other items from the barrels was complete. Dr Gilbert telephoned the State Coroner, Wayne Chivell, to notify him that the remains of eight people had been found. He later compiled a detailed list:

Barrel A:

Total mass: 113.5 kg.

Contents: One intact male body wearing a jumper. Tattoos noted on chest. This body was placed in a body bag designated as A1.

Two matted lumps of hair.

Four slabs of skin and underlying muscle.

Two disarticulated femurs with traces of muscle and tendon tissue attached.

One disarticulated right lower leg with the foot missing.

One disarticulated left lower leg with partially disarticulated left foot.

These items were placed in a body bag designated A2.

Also within barrel A were pieces of plastic, electrical wire and numerous rubber gloves.

Barrel B:

Total mass: 155.5 kg.

Contents: One clothed male body with tattooed arms.

This body was placed in a body bag designated B.

Other items found in the barrel included part of a syringe, a plastic bag and a perforated black plastic mat was found at the base of the drum. These items were placed in separate labelled plastic bags.

Barrel C:

Total mass: 119 kg.

Contents: Male body, handcuffed, legs tied, plastic bags over head and legs. Soft tissue loss noted around one of the knees with the corresponding patella (kneecap) loose in the barrel.

The body was placed in a body bag designated C.

Barrel D:

Total mass: 168.5 kg.

Contents: Clothed male body missing lower legs and feet.

Yellow tape around head. Rope around neck.

This body was placed in a body bag designated D1.

Left and right lower legs, each with attached feet. Each foot bore a sock.

A loose disarticulated left foot.

These items were placed in a body bag designated D2.

Clothed male body missing the left foot but otherwise intact. Rope around neck.

Earring in left ear.

This body was placed in a body bag designated D3.

Barrel E:

Total mass: 163.5 kg.

Contents: A complete female body, clothed, with tape around the mouth and rope and fabric tape intertwined loosely around the legs.

This body was placed in a body bag designated E.

Barrel F:

Total mass: 192.5 kg.

Contents: A complete male body dressed in underpants. There was skin and soft tissue loss over the right lower thigh and right knee joint.

The barrel also contained a rectangular piece of skin and subcutaneous tissue corresponding in size to the right thigh defect.

These items were placed in a body bag designated F1.

Male body missing legs and with incisions in anterior abdominal wall. Tape around head. Rope around neck. A loose right foot.

These items were placed in a body bag designated F2.

Other items located in the barrel included loose rubber gloves and the barrel of a syringe with attached needle. These items were placed in separate labelled bags.

ELEVEN

The adrenaline was still pumping, and it was just as well: it was 4.30 a.m. when Paul Schramm and his team arrived back in Adelaide. The drive from Snowtown had seemed to take forever and the briefing was only thirty minutes away.

Dozens of officers had been recalled to duty. Many had been on days off; one was due to start holidays. All had been told to report to Major Crime by 5 a.m. and few were told why. The briefing began right on time and Paul Schramm did the talking. He gave a synopsis of the case, explaining how detectives had linked the disappearances of five people and the investigation pointed to at least three suspects. Next Schramm outlined the chain of events which had led to the previous day's discovery at Snowtown. It was likely, he added, that the barrels contained the remains of more murder victims than police had expected.

There was an intense silence as the video footage filmed inside the Snowtown bank vault was played on a large television. Eyes were fixed firmly on the screen as the camera panned across the room, revealing its sinister contents. A lid was screwed off one of the barrels, revealing human remains.

Since the discovery, surveillance officers – known as 'dogs' – had been watching the suspects. This morning, Schramm instructed, John Bunting, Robert Wagner and

Mark Haydon were to be arrested. Each was to be charged with one count of murder, because it was still unclear how many bodies had been found at Snowtown. The single charge would be enough to keep the men in custody.

Three teams of police would execute simultaneous raids on the suspects' homes. Two detectives in each team would be responsible for the arrest; the others would search for evidence.

Shortly after 6 a.m. the teams rolled out of the city. The surveillance crews were ordered out as the arrest teams moved in.

It was 6.47 a.m. when the detectives arrived at John Bunting's house, 49 Bundarra Crescent, in the northern suburb of Craigmore. Veteran investigators Bob Stapleton and Kym Presgrave were to make the arrest and it was Stapleton who knocked on the door, a tape recorder clutched in his hand to capture every word. James Vlassakis answered the door.

'Good morning. Police officers. I would like to speak to John Bunting, please.' The detectives walked into the hallway, where Bunting appeared.

'John Bunting, we are police officers. I'm Detective Stapleton, Detective Presgrave, we are from Major Crime. We are investigating the disappearance of Clinton Trezise, Barry Lane, Elizabeth Haydon, Ray Davies and Suzanne Allen. We believe that you might be able to help us with our inquiries. I'm now arresting you on suspicion of the murder at this stage of an unidentified person, body found in a drum in a disused banking premises at Snowtown yesterday, the 20th of May 1999. I am now required to advise you of your rights and to advise you that anything you say will be recorded and may be given in evidence.'

If Bunting was shocked, he didn't show it.

'You are entitled to make a telephone call in the presence of a member of the police force to a nominated relative or friend to advise them of your whereabouts. Do you understand that?'

There was no response.

'Do you wish to make a telephone call? Can you answer yes or no, please?'

'No, I don't wish to make a call.'

'Do you understand your right to make a call, can you speak up, please?'

'Yeah.'

'You are entitled to have a solicitor, relative or friend present during any interrogation or investigation while in custody. Do you understand that? Can you please answer?'

'Yeah.'

'You are entitled to refrain from answering any questions while in custody. Do you understand that?'

'Yeah.'

'We will be leaving here in a moment and going into the Adelaide police station where we will speak with you further. At the completion of that you will be entitled to make an application for bail. Do you understand that?'

'Yep.'

'Right, if you just move this way, these other officers will conduct a search of the premises. Do you want some shoes? Will you just empty your pockets, please?'

Bunting emptied the pockets of the jeans he was wearing.

'Right, do you have anything else on your person?'

'Nah.'

'We will just search you, just to make sure, just for safety reasons, do you understand?'

After being taken to the toilet, a handcuffed John Bunting was led to an unmarked police car. As Detective Presgrave drove back to the city, Detective Stapleton sat in the back seat next to their prisoner.

In the nearby suburb of Elizabeth Grove, it was Robert Wagner who answered the knock at his door. Detective Craig Patterson told him he was under arrest and informed him of his rights.

'Do you wish to exercise any of those rights, Robert?'

'Yep.'

'What would you like to exercise?'

'I'm not saying anything.'

Further north, in Smithfield Plains, Mark Haydon also had little to say when Detectives Greg Stone and Steve McCoy arrested him. Like the others, he was handcuffed and taken to a waiting car.

Less than an hour after their arrests, all three prisoners had arrived at the Adelaide police station, where each was seated in a separate interview room. The interview rooms were small; a table against one wall and chairs at either side. Each room was equipped with video and audio recording equipment. At 7.45 a.m. Detective Stapleton activated the video camera and tape recorders in the room where John Bunting was sitting. Detective Presgrave was with them.

'Mr Bunting, a short time ago when we entered the room and I indicated to you to move closer to the microphone you said to me that you don't want to do an interview, is that correct?'

'Yeah.'

Stapleton then summarised the morning's events and offered to replay the tape recording of Bunting's arrest. Bunting didn't respond.

'Is that a refusal to answer my question?'

'I told you I'm not doing this. I would like my phone call now. I wish to ring Legal Aid.'

'Right, I will organise a phone call for you straightaway.'

Several attempts were made to contact the government's Legal Services Commission to find Bunting a lawyer. He was again told of his rights before being taken from the interview room to the police city watch house. At 8.19 a.m. John Justin Bunting was formally charged with one count of murder.

At 9 a.m., Detective Stapleton led Bunting into the police medical examination room. Bunting was cautioned that their conversation was being recorded. The police medical examiner, Dr Ernest Flock, took over.

'Okay Mr Bunting, I'm Dr Flock, as the officer said, and I've been asked to just do two things, that is take a sample of your blood, all right, and also take some hair samples. This will be for comparison purposes as part of the investigation. Right, now, just a couple of things I have to ask you. You don't have to answer them if you don't want to. Making sure of your surname, all right, Bunting, is that correct? And John Justin?'

'Right,' Bunting replied and nodded his head.

'Can I have your date of birth, please?'

'Four, nine, sixty-six.'

'We will be taking blood with a needle from one of the arms, so I have to know if you suffer from any bleeding or, like, haemophilia, like where you bruise or bleed easy?'

'No.'

'Fine, we will just pull your chair a bit closer to here and then we will get you to rest your arm, get a couple of things ready and then we're in business.'

Bunting then turned to Detective Stapleton. 'Do I have to give a blood sample?'

'Yes, you are required to give a blood sample and we are able to use as much force as necessary to obtain that sample.'

'It's not necessary, I'm just asking.'

'And I'm just advising you.'

'Why are you here?'

'I have to be present.'

'You're not the doctor.'

'I'm required to be present during the examination.'

Dr Flock took the blood from Bunting's arm, placed a small dressing over the wound and asked Bunting to hold it down.

'Next we will just pluck a few hairs out from your head at the back. It's a bit uncomfortable but it's not bad. We need about ten at least.'

Bunting's blood and hair samples were placed in a refrigerator and would later be used to obtain his DNA profile and, perhaps, vital evidence. Robert Wagner, a lawyer with him, objected to his medical examination but offered no physical resistance. He too had blood and hair samples taken.

Mark Haydon's examination was more thorough, Dr Flock taking not only blood and hair, but also scrapings from under his fingernails and toenails. He was also asked to remove his clothes and place his T-shirt and shorts into separate bags before being given white paper overalls to wear.

By 11.43 a.m. – almost five hours after the teams of police had swooped on their homes – Bunting, Wagner and Haydon had been charged with the murder of a person unknown. All three had refused to answer questions about the crimes they were suspected of committing.

★   ★   ★

Another target of the morning's operation was John Bunting's de facto, Elizabeth Harvey. Police suspected she had helped Bunting steal money from the missing people's bank accounts and might have knowledge of their murders.

Harvey had been in bed when police arrived at the home she shared with Bunting. Two detectives asked her to go with them to the local police station and she agreed.

Though not under arrest, Harvey was interviewed by detectives Jennifer O'Donohue and Malcolm Williams for more than two hours. Harvey told them she'd been in a relationship with Bunting since 1994 and now he was caring for her as she died of cancer. She identified Robert Wagner as a friend of Bunting's.

Harvey told the detectives she had four sons, but hadn't seen her eldest, Troy, for close to eight months. She confirmed that David Johnson was her stepson and was visibly shocked when told his wallet had been found in the Snowtown bank vault. He could be one of the victims.

Detective Williams listed the names of the missing people police had been seeking. Harvey admitted to knowing three of them – Barry Lane, Elizabeth Haydon and Suzanne Allen – but not Ray Davies or Clinton Trezise.

'The fact that I've told you that we believe these people have been murdered, and we believe yesterday we found their bodies and that Bunting and Wagner are involved in this, does that surprise you?'

Harvey shook her head: 'Um, I don't believe it. I'm sorry, I just can't, I think you're barking up the wrong tree. I honestly do, I can't – I, I'm stressed out about – I'm not, I'm not amazed, I just don't believe it.'

'If I was to tell you he [Bunting] has been videotaped at different money outlets ... getting money paid into these missing persons' accounts, they were on social security benefits ... and he's used their cards to access their accounts —'

'I wouldn't know anything about it.'

'Did you ever ... change Suzanne Allen's pension type or address?'

'No.'

Harvey's denials were emphatic, but she was lying. When detectives searched her handbag they found a letter addressed to Suzanne Allen which had been sent to a house at Murray Bridge where Harvey and Bunting had lived. The letter was from Centrelink, the wellfare and employment office.

Detective Williams went on the offensive: 'Can you explain to me what you are doing with that document?'

'No I can't, sorry.' Harvey was squirming.

'Can't or don't want to?'

'I don't know.'

'You sure you haven't kept this for identification?'

'No.'

'You sure you haven't been obtaining Suzanne Allen's benefits?'

'No, I haven't.'

'Knowing that she's been murdered?'

After the interview was over, the detectives were driving Elizabeth Harvey home when she decided to change her story. They were back in the police interview room within minutes. This time there were no denials, but no admissions of murder.

'I was taking you home when you said something about John Bunting coming home and saying that he'd found Suzanne Allen in the bath and she was dead. Could you just reiterate or go over what you told me in the car?'

'I only very vaguely knew Sue, and he [Bunting] came home and said that he found Sue dead, slumped over the bath. I asked him what he was doing around there and he said he was robbing her place while she was in Tasmania and that he and Robert [Wagner] came into the house and Sue was slumped over the bath, dead.'

Harvey explained that when she asked Bunting what they'd done with Suzanne Allen's body, he told her to 'shut up'.

'I asked him if he notified the police and he said no, because he would have got lumbered with the robbery.'

Elizabeth Harvey's confession was extensive. She told the detectives that after Bunting had found Suzanne Allen dead – apparently of natural causes – her property was stolen and sold off. Bunting kept Allen's credit union card but couldn't steal money from her account because he didn't have the personal identification number (PIN). By snapping the card and impersonating Suzanne Allen, Harvey obtained a new card and PIN. For the next twelve months she stole Allen's pension, which Centrelink paid into the bank account every fortnight. After that, Harvey gave the card back to Bunting.

By the end of her interview, police had enough to charge Elizabeth Harvey with fraud. However there was nothing to implicate her in the murders and she had emerged as a vital witness. Harvey was free to go – at least for now.

Media crews had been perched on ladders for close to six hours; nobody wanted to surrender their position. From their respective vantage points, television cameramen and newspaper photographers could see through the mesh and razor wire into a secure courtyard. It was through this area that prisoners were marched from police cells – the city watch house – to the Adelaide Magistrates Court.

The media was eagerly awaiting the court appearance of three men. Court documents had revealed their names: John Justin Bunting, Robert Joe Wagner and Mark Ray Haydon. The trio had been arrested early that morning. The arrests followed the discovery of bodies in barrels at an old bank the day before – Thursday, 20 March 1999 – at a place called Snowtown. The small town north of Adelaide was by now crawling with police and news crews.

It was a little before three-thirty in the afternoon when the watch house door swung open and the cameras began flashing. Each of the men was handcuffed at the front, Wagner first to emerge followed by Bunting and Haydon. Their looks were sullen, although both Bunting and Wagner allowed themselves a glance at the media pack behind the wire. The look on Bunting's face made it seem as though, ever so slightly, he had enjoyed the moment.

Within minutes the trio stood in the high-security dock of Court Seventeen. Reinforced glass separated them from the rest of the room; guards were standing inside and out.

The men looked at the magistrate as he read the charge aloud: 'You are charged with the murder of a person unknown between August 1, 1993, and May 20, 1999.' The magistrate's voice was steady, the packed courtroom silent. The police were still reeling from their discovery the day before.

Within four minutes the hearing was over. As they were led to a waiting prison van, Bunting and Wagner smiled pleasantly at their guards. If they were worried about their predicament, it didn't show.

TWELVE

At first, John Bunting had been like a father to James Vlassakis, arriving just as Jamie's life was in crisis. The teenager's family was impoverished; his mother a psychiatric mess addicted to drugs and gambling. Bunting was Jamie's saviour, offering protection to a boy who'd been the repeated victim of sexual abuse from his own father.

However, as time passed, John Bunting's darker side emerged and Jamie became frightened. Bunting would rant incessantly about paedophiles, describing them as 'dirties' who deserved to die. Jamie watched in horror as Bunting killed animals for pleasure, some of them skinned alive.

The teenager stood by, knowingly, as Bunting's prey became human. Eventually, through a combination of fear and weakness, Jamie joined the killing spree and thus became a murderer, turning to drugs in an effort to forget.

It was James Vlassakis who answered the knock at the door the day Bunting was arrested. As Jamie watched Bunting being led away in handcuffs, his stomach was churning. His mother, too, had been taken away for questioning. Sooner or later, Jamie believed, the police would be back for him.

Distraught, he turned to his friend Wally Fitzgerald for help:

He rang my place just after 7 a.m., he was crying and said that his mother and John had been arrested for fraud and murder. He wanted me to go and get his heroin. I thought he was bullshitting so I hung up.

At about 8 a.m. he again rang up and said that he was coming round in a taxi. He arrived about 8.30 a.m. He came in, I sent the kids off to school, asked him what was going on, he was crying, he said that his mother and John had been arrested for fraud and murder. I made him a cup of coffee; I asked him if it was true. He said it was.

During his emotional outpouring, Jamie told Wally much of what he knew about the murders. Among his revelations was that bodies were buried in the back yard of a house where John Bunting had once lived.

The following day Wally Fitzgerald telephoned the police Crime Stoppers line, alerting them to the secret suburban gravesite.

The ground-penetrating radar looked more like a common lawnmower: a wheel-mounted device which, when passed over a section of ground, detects disturbances in the earth, indicating whether or not something is buried there. Similar technology had been used five years earlier to help pinpoint nine bodies entombed in the concrete foundations of the house of English serial killers Fred and Rosemary West in Cromwell Street, Gloucester. The 'House of Horrors' case had received worldwide attention.

It was a Sunday morning, 23 May 1999, when teams of police converged on the small, unremarkable home in Adelaide's northern suburbs. Curious neighbours and media formed a crowd in the street.

The address was 203 Waterloo Corner Road, Salisbury

North. It was a house where John Bunting had once lived. The police were looking for bodies.

With the assistance of State Emergency Service (SES) volunteers a large tent was erected in the back yard, covering the area of interest to detectives. In a corner of the yard, under 7 centimetres of earth, was a concrete slab on which a rainwater tank had once stood. The technician slowly wheeled the radar over the suspect site as apprehensive police watched on. Waiting. The results were encouraging – there was something down there.

Detective Sergeant Brian Swan was in charge of the operation. At 11.30 a.m. he gave the order to start digging. Police and SES workers used crowbars, sledgehammers and spades to break up the concrete slab. Getting through the earth below was only marginally easier.

Almost five hours later, at a depth of 1.37 metres, police caught sight of a green garbage bag. Delicate digging revealed ten more. One of the bags was opened, releasing the distinctive smell of rotting flesh and revealing what appeared to be human remains. Each garbage bag was marked for identification, photographed, and delivered to the Forensic Science Centre.

The next morning, forensic pathologist Dr Roger Byard began his examination. The eleven bags were first X-rayed, then opened one by one.

Inside one bag was a human torso – the chest and abdomen. Tissue and skeletal muscle were still present, along with some internal organs. Dr Byard noted that the overlying skin had been removed, with the exception of three small areas. The head had been crudely cut off, the arms and legs also sliced away. The chest was compressed and the genitals were missing.

Another of the bags contained two feet cut off at the

ankles, and a head. Tangled within the medium-length black hair was a piece of blue nylon rope. The severed legs, arms and hands were in other bags. Dr Byard concluded that the limbs, like the torso, had been 'defleshed':

The body had been disarticulated through the joints, most likely with a knife, with no evidence of sawing of bones. The defleshing of the limbs and torso was also most likely done with a knife, as several of the skin fragments demonstrated clean incised edges.

Reconstructing the body indicated that, apart from autolytic and possibly previous surgically removed internal organs, no other body parts were missing. The limbs were symmetrical and appropriate for the size of the torso. The hands and feet were also symmetrical. This indicated that the body parts were most likely derived from a single body. The body was an adult white female.

Three days after their first discovery, police returned to 203 Waterloo Corner Road. Children climbed a tree to peer over a fence, traffic slowed to a crawl and a crowd again gathered; locals were joined by a frenzied media throng, hungry for another instalment in this sensational story. At one point even a catering van stopped outside, cashing in on the morbid spectacle.

In the back yard police used a backhoe to excavate the same area where the woman's remains had already been unearthed. Detectives believed they would find another body if they dug deeper.

Almost 2 metres further down, a skeleton was uncovered. Crime scene officers began taking photographs as bones were carefully removed and placed in clear plastic evidence bags. Detective Patterson, wearing long gloves, was given the tedious task of sifting through the dirt. He used a sieve to ensure even the smallest bones were found. Behind him Detective Swan, a clipboard cradled in his left arm, logged every piece of evidence.

Dr Ross James, another forensic pathologist, examined the skeletal remains the following day:

> The remains consisted entirely of essentially dried skeletal material apart from a hood of a parka, khaki in colour, covered with dirt and encompassing the skull vault.
>
> The skeletal materials were those of an adult male and the skeletal tissue was essentially complete. There were no personal effects or other items of clothing present.
>
> The bones were all dry and clean, without soft tissue or any obvious odour of decay. The mouth contained a complete set of teeth with numerous amalgam fillings.
>
> Cause of death is not apparent. The bones are free of injury and no ligatures were present around the neck.

There were no visible injuries nor mutilations. Dr James found no restraints on the skeleton, and concluded that the man had died at least two years before, possibly more.

In the days after Bunting's arrest, James Vlassakis and his mother were feeling the pressure. The teenager was struggling to come to terms with his guilt, while Elizabeth had endured hours of police questioning.

Wally Fitzgerald, a petty criminal, put them in touch with his lawyer, whom they met on the same day detectives began digging at Waterloo Corner Road. Within hours the lawyer had contacted police. His clients would tell all, but they wanted immunity.

A solicitor at his side, the interview with James Vlassakis

began at 5.32 p.m. on Monday, 24 May 1999. The detectives were Steve McCoy and Greg Stone. It was McCoy who outlined the terms of the meeting:

> We will not be issuing you with a caution and, as a result, the statement you make will not be used against you in any proceeding. Once this statement has been completed it will be forwarded to the Director of Public Prosecutions. This statement will then be checked and assessed, for example, as to the accuracy and completeness in light of all the evidence available. It is only then that a decision will be made by the Director of Public Prosecutions as to whether or not full immunity will be granted to you.

The harrowing interview spanned ten days. Throughout it Vlassakis was visibly distressed – often crying, sometimes physically ill.

Police had discovered eight bodies in Snowtown, but Vlassakis detailed twelve murders, some of which he'd been told about, others he'd taken part in. During a break the confessions became too much and the nineteen-year-old overdosed on heroin and almost died. He had been using drugs heavily and it seemed the only way out.

The murders Vlassakis recounted were bizarre and ritualistic. Victims had been chosen, then killed. They had been tortured, sometimes with music playing in the background. Some were given electric shocks, burned, injected. Toes were crushed with pliers. Those about to die had been forced to subjugate themselves to their attackers – refer to them as 'Lord' or 'Master'.

Vlassakis described how Bunting and Wagner delighted in the pain and suffering; how they feverishly anticipated the kill. Bunting liked to stare into his victims' eyes.

James Vlassakis's off-the-record confessions ended on the afternoon of 2 June 1999. At 5.40 p.m. he was arrested, then taken to the police cells, searched and formally charged with murder. Vlassakis was medically examined – blood and hair samples were taken – then transferred to a secure ward at Adelaide's Glenside Psychiatric Hospital.

The following day, having attempted suicide twice in a week, Vlassakis was moved to the Correctional Service Department's secure psychiatric facility, James Nash House. It would be another ten months before the young man was officially told he would not be granted immunity.

The revelations made by James Vlassakis could not be used as evidence against him. Still, they were invaluable. The information he had volunteered provided police with a kind of a road map for their investigation.

Indeed, it was information from Vlassakis which had prompted police to revisit 203 Waterloo Corner Road, making a second discovery of human remains.

More importantly, Vlassakis had detailed a dozen murders – and provided a list of victims' names.

Detectives from Task Force Chart – as the operation had been named – were now in the midst of the single biggest criminal investigation in Australian history. They were to follow countless leads, interview thousands of witnesses and collect volumes of evidence.

Over the next three years, and even as the accused stood trial, a team of dedicated police worked tirelessly in their search for answers. They would leave no stone unturned – every fact was needed so justice could be done and the victims' families could know the terrible truth.

What emerged was a horrid story. It was beyond most rational people's imaginations.

PART TWO

THE MURDERS

THIRTEEN

James Vlassakis will never forget the look of delight on John Bunting's face. It was as though the thrill of the kill had come rushing back.

The pair was watching television, a true-crime show called *Australia's Most Wanted*. This episode detailed the discovery of a skeleton at a place called Lower Light. The young man had been murdered several years before and the case remained unsolved. As he spoke, Bunting could hardly contain his excitement.

'That's my handiwork!'

Clinton Douglas Trezise was the first of the serial killing victims; he was murdered in August 1992 by John Bunting. The scene of the crime was the lounge room of Bunting's home at 203 Waterloo Corner Road, Salisbury North. The motive had almost certainly been Bunting's warped hatred of homosexuals.

Bunting bludgeoned the teenager to death with a hammer, caving in the back of his skull. Forensic evidence indicated that Clinton was lying face down on the floor as the blows rained down on him. The attack was so ferocious that the front of the victim's skull was also shattered. A fracture to his left hand suggested that he'd tried to protect himself in his final moments of life.

With the killing done, Bunting wrapped the victim's body in garbage bags and then enlisted the help of two friends: Robert Wagner and Barry Lane. The body was loaded into Barry Lane's station wagon.

Unaware of the day's events, Bunting's then wife, Veronika, went with her husband to Lane and Wagner's house – supposedly for dinner:

> John, Robert and Barry were talking. They were talking in the lounge room when the three of them got up and Barry asked me if I could look after the dogs and cats ... while he could go off somewhere with John and Robert. Before Barry left, he locked me inside the house. I saw them walking off towards our house at 203 Waterloo Corner Road.

Within days a terrified Barry Lane had visited Veronika Bunting to tell her what had happened. But Lane cautioned Veronika against asking her husband too many questions. She ignored his advice – curiosity had got the better of her:

> John told me parts of what they did. John said that he took someone up to Lower Light and buried them in a hole. His name was Clinton Trezise and he was a friend of Barry and Robert's. He met him at Barry and Robert's house and took an instant disliking to him.
>
> I have never told anybody else about this conversation as I didn't want to get killed. I believed that if I did tell somebody, John would kill me.

Around the time of his murder Clinton Trezise had been leading a solitary life. A slightly built lad with brown hair, a freckled face and crooked teeth, the only striking thing about the eighteen-year-old was the brightly coloured pants he often wore. At the time they were known as 'Happy Pants'.

Openly homosexual, Clinton lived by himself in a small house in Adelaide's northern suburbs, his only furniture a kitchen table, bed and portable television.

Loneliness was nothing new to Clinton. The young man had few friends and only occasional contact with his family. Clinton's parents, Doug and Marilyn, had divorced when he was three. With younger brother Scott, Clinton had been placed into foster care while the boys' sister, Sherie, stayed with their mother. Clinton spent his childhood with other families, barely knowing his own.

In his teens Clinton attended an adult re-entry school in a bid to get his life on track. He formed a bond with classmate named Steven, the pair spending much of their time 'hanging out' in the city. The boys eventually became flatmates, but their arrangement came to an abrupt end when Clinton made a sexual advance towards his friend.

At about the same time Clinton had come to know two other men – a couple who lived in the nearby suburb of Salisbury North. The older man was Barry Lane; his young partner, Robert Wagner. One neighbour remembers Clinton visiting regularly.

I remember that Barry introduced Clinton as someone he was looking after for someone else, rather than looking after for himself. Clinton didn't say hardly anything and seemed quite shy ... I thought Clinton might have been some sort of street kid they were helping out.

After a month I hadn't seen him and I asked Barry where he had gone. I can't remember the exact words, but Barry said something like 'it didn't work out'.

Barry Lane's interest in this teenager was almost certainly a sexual one. Lane needed a new, submissive partner because he could no longer have his way with Robert Wagner.

Wagner had turned against Lane – he had become John Bunting's protégé and now shared Bunting's extreme views on paedophiles and, ironically, homosexuals.

Tragically, Clinton's association with Barry Lane most likely cost him his life. It had drawn him to the attention of John Bunting – and Bunting didn't like what he saw.

Ray Davies had exhibited unusual sexual behaviour from an early age. At first it was harmless: playing with his sister's dolls, wearing her clothes. But his peculiarities attracted attention at school, where he was constantly mocked and harassed by classmates.

Born James Leslie Davies (he later changed his name), Ray's parents were intellectually disabled. Those who knew Ray regarded him as 'slow' but 'cunning'. He spent much of his childhood living in country South Australia, being cared for by his aunt. It was she who discovered how profoundly perverted the boy she called Jamie had become:

> I treated James as my son; I used to call him Jamie. So the first time I realised that Jamie had a sexual problem was when he was about thirteen or fourteen years of age; he was in high school.
>
> This one night the family came around to my house and I was told that Jamie had been teased at school and was upset and didn't want to come around to my place, so I got on my pushbike and rode around to where they lived.
>
> When I walked around the back of the house I caught Jamie playing with the family's dog; he looked as though he was having sex with it.

I told him he was a dirty boy and to get to my place straightaway.

By the time he was twenty Ray Davies was a petty criminal, with convictions for stealing and assault. And there was another incident involving a dog, for which he was charged with indecent behaviour.

In 1989 Ray moved to Adelaide's northern suburbs, where he shuffled from one address to the other. At one time he lived with a gay couple named Barry Lane and Robert Wagner, often visiting local homosexual haunts with Lane.

Through Barry Lane, Ray Davies met a woman named Suzanne Allen. She lived nearby and the pair soon formed a relationship. Ray and Sue moved in together and became engaged to be married. Ray, however, continued his sexual liaisons with other men, including Barry Lane, and by 1993 the relationship with Sue was over. The couple remained friends, though, and Sue allowed Ray to live in a caravan in her back yard.

Still, Ray's sexual behaviour was a problem. Neighbours complained that he would hide in bushes and masturbate as school children walked by.

Sue Allen's next serious boyfriend was John Bunting; Bunting was also involved with Elizabeth Harvey. He lived up the road from Sue and would visit regularly, often with his mate Robert Wagner.

It didn't take long for Bunting and Wagner to learn of Ray Davies's lewd behaviour towards local children. Barry Lane had also warned them that Davies was a paedophile.

Ray Davies's fate was sealed the day after Christmas, 1995, when he was accused of molesting two young boys who had been staying at Sue Allen's house. Devastated, Sue ordered Ray to leave. She almost certainly told John Bunting what Davies had done.

Within days, Ray Davies had disappeared.

Handcuffed and terrified, Ray Davies was forced into the boot of the car. As he slammed the boot shut, John Bunting warned Ray Davies to 'be good'. Robert Wagner started the car as Bunting jumped in. Their destination was a little over two hours away – a small town called Bakara.

When the car pulled up outside the old house, Bunting knew the coast would be clear. He was renting the Bakara house, living there with Elizabeth Harvey and her four boys. The family had gone back to Adelaide for Christmas and New Year, so the place was empty.

Bunting and Wagner grabbed their prey from the boot. They marched him, still handcuffed, into the bathroom and forced him into the bath. It was to become their murderous routine. Ray Davies was savagely beaten about the groin and thighs with a metal pole. Bunting would later brag that his victim's testicles swelled to 'the size of golf balls' by the time the torture was over. Struggling to walk, Ray was put back in the boot.

It was late morning, perhaps lunchtime, when they returned to Adelaide. Bunting still rented the house at 203 Waterloo Corner Road and Elizabeth Harvey was inside. 'We've got a present for you,' Bunting said as he walked in. 'It's in the car.'

Harvey watched in stunned silence as Ray Davies was dragged through the door:

He was obviously in a lot of pain, he was handcuffed. I couldn't think ... they took him into the bathroom and they started yelling and screaming at him. Calling him a faggot and a baby rapist and things like that.

Ray was then forced into a bedroom. It was the same room where his name was displayed on Bunting's paedophile chart: the Wall of Spiders.

Bunting called for Elizabeth Harvey to 'come in'. She and Robert Wagner then wrapped car jumper leads around Ray's neck and twisted them until he was dead. Starved of air, their lifeless victim slumped to the floor. Bunting turned to Harvey, smiling: 'Do you like your present?'

Elizabeth Harvey did not know why she had joined in. Perhaps it was fear of Bunting. She had seen what he was capable of, after all. Or perhaps it had been anger over her children's abuse at the hands of men like Ray Davies. Whatever the reason, she too was now a killer.

Ray Davies's body was thrown into a large hole in the back yard at 203 Waterloo Corner Road. The hole, under a brick stand built for the rainwater tank, had been dug by John Bunting.

Originally the deep chasm had been intended as some kind of underground room. Such a secret place had been a strange childhood fantasy of John Bunting's; lights and a ladder had even been installed.

The hole seemed the perfect place to dump a body. Bunting would later joke that Davies was 'still holding his balls' as he was thrown in.

To cover their murderous tracks, Bunting and Wagner later told Sue Allen a story to explain why Ray Davies had suddenly disappeared, leaving behind his caravan and possessions. The killers wanted it to appear as though they had punished Ray Davies for what he had done and now he was too scared to return. The conversation was overheard by Sue's daughter. She recalled that Robert Wagner was there at the time:

> I heard John say to ... Mum [Sue Allen] words to the effect – 'We took Ray for a drive in the car.' John said while he was driving, 'Robert was pounding him down and trying to keep him down so that no one could see what was going on in the back seat.' He made hand movements indicating punching down. It sounded like Ray was on the floor of the car. He said that they 'dropped him off in the middle of the scrub somewhere and made him walk back towards town'. They didn't say if he was hurt or bleeding or anything. John was laughing about it. Robert had a big cheesy smile on his face. He didn't say much apart from saying it was really good.

At the time of the Ray Davies murder, Bunting's affair with Sue Allen was going strong. Distance was Bunting's protection: his de facto and her children were living in the country, first at Bakara, then at Murray Bridge.

Still, Bunting rented the house at 203 Waterloo Corner Road, where he and his de facto family would sometimes stay.

However, Bunting broke off his relationship with Sue Allen sometime in 1996. One of Sue's daughters tried unsuccessfully to get them back together:

> Mum used to give me notes to give him. They were about how she still loved him and missed him and wanted him back.
>
> I know Mum would often drive past his place. John

knew about this and mentioned it to me that she was driving past virtually every day.

He did tell me to tell her to stop the notes and to stop driving past.

One of the notes, a lipstick-marked two-page love letter, was discovered later by police:

Dear John,

I am finding it hard to be away from you all the time. I wish that you could stay with me for good because I love you so much … I hope you are feeling the same way about me.

So my darling John, please do not take too long to come back to me, I will always wait for you.

The letter was signed 'all my love, Suzanne'.

Sue's attention was becoming an irritation to Bunting, however, and their relationship had become hostile. It was possible, too, that she knew too much. Bunting had bragged to Sue Allen about the time he and Robert Wagner took Ray Davies 'for a drive'. And Davies had not been seen since.

Sue Allen's disappearance was first noticed by her brother, John, in November 1996. Her usually tidy home looked as though it had been ransacked, much of her furniture was gone and Sue's starving pets had been collected by the RSPCA. Not long after her brother reported her missing, Sue's car also disappeared.

Despite the stories told by Bunting and Wagner, it appears almost certain that Sue Allen was murdered in her own home, 3 Ghent Street, Salisbury North, by Robert

Wagner and John Bunting. She was most likely strangled, as Ray Davies had been.

Rather than brag about the latest killing, Bunting concocted a story to explain Sue Allen's death. The first to hear the far-fetched tale was James Vlassakis. Living with mates at the time, Vlassakis had gone to Murray Bridge to visit Bunting and his mother. Inside their house he had noticed Sue Allen's belongings:

> I queried Mum. I said, 'This is Sue's stuff', and she said, 'No it's not.'
>
> That night I had a conversation with John about it . . . he just told me that . . . he was knocking on Sue's front door. There was no answer. He went round the back or something, got in the house and she was lying on the bathroom floor. He said that he had to open a door, couldn't actually get the door open because she was in the way, and when he got the door open she was dead, absolutely naked, dead on the floor in the bathroom.
>
> I got told she died of natural causes.

While claiming they had found Suzanne Allen already dead, Bunting and Wagner were only too happy to detail for Vlassakis how they had 'sliced and diced' Sue Allen, dismembering her body in her bathtub:

> Robert used the head as a puppet and told John to kiss it, kiss the head . . .

Sue Allen's body parts were placed into garbage bags and taken to Bunting's house at 203 Waterloo Corner Road. The bags were thrown into the same hole where Ray Davies had been buried a year before. Later, it was filled in.

★   ★   ★

After Sue Allen's murder, Bunting and Wagner spread their series of lies to explain her disappearance. Unlike the first two victims, Sue had a network of family and friends and they were worried. One such friend was Carol Parker:

> Sometime after Sue was reported missing, John [Bunting] and his mate Robert came around to my place to visit and told me Sue got bashed up in the face. I asked why and he said because she hadn't paid money back she borrowed from two guys so she could fix her car. John ... said she borrowed a thousand dollars from these two guys and they wanted their money ... then said to me that Sue had told him that a Ray Davies was one of the guys that had bashed her up and that she was now in hiding.
>
> Everything John told me that happened to Sue, his mate Robert would agree with him.

The false stories continued during a later visit:

> I remember them saying Sue was living somewhere in Gawler and that she had met some young guy in his twenties and they got married. They used to tell me this all the time.

Within months of Sue's brother reporting her missing, investigators discovered that Sue's pension was still being paid into her bank account by Centrelink. The cash withdrawals continued and bank records listed an address for Sue Allen. The address was John Bunting's, so he was contacted by police.

Bunting's lies continued: he told missing persons investigators that Sue had been staying with him but had recently moved interstate with her new lover, 'Andy'. He claimed Sue was embroiled in a family conflict and did not want to be found. At the time, the story seemed plausible.

Police told Sue Allen's family that her pension was still active, so all seemed fine, but when her daughter Tammy turned to Centrelink for help to contact her mum, she was told privacy regulations prevented them giving her any such assistance. Sue's sister, Joan, wrote letters to Centrelink asking that a message be passed onto her sibling. There was no reply.

FOURTEEN

John Bunting's killing spree was supposedly born of his depraved fury at paedophiles and homosexuals. In his deluded mind, they were one and the same. This was the initial motive for murder, but blood lust soon took over. John Bunting loved to kill – he loved the power.

Clinton Trezise was murdered because he was homosexual; Ray Davies was chosen because he was a paedophile. But Suzanne Allen had become a nuisance who knew too much.

Bunting not only revelled in his crimes, he included others: Mark Haydon, Barry Lane and Robert Wagner. Lane was a paedophile whom Bunting befriended to extract information about others who preyed on children.

Between Bunting and Wagner, however, a kinship developed – both had been sexually abused as children.

Robert Wagner escaped the hold Barry Lane had over him, only to be lured by another evil: John Bunting. Wagner became Bunting's 'muscle', his right-hand man. Wagner, too, enjoyed the killing and it was he who had strangled Ray Davies and, most likely, Suzanne Allen. Wagner earned the nickname 'Papa Smurf' because he turned his victims blue, the same colour as the cartoon characters the Smurfs.

By 1997 Robert Wagner had renounced his

homosexuality. He refused to even speak of his relationship with Barry Lane and became enraged if it was mentioned by anyone else.

Wagner now even had a fiancée, Sally Brown★. The couple shared a home with her three children and late that year had a child together – a baby boy.

Wagner developed an interest too in his community, joining the local school council and the Country Fire Service, where he trained as a volunteer firefighter. Other volunteers gave him the nickname Lurch. Said one:

> He never became a friend of mine because I found him strange. He was quiet, always looked through people and was a racist. He openly admitted to bashing 'poofters' and didn't like Asians and blacks.

On one occasion two other CFS volunteers noticed handcuffs and thumbcuffs in Robert Wagner's toolbox. When asked why he had them, Wagner replied: 'You can't be too careful these days.'

Robert Wagner disliked Michael Gardiner from the start. He was effeminate and obviously homosexual, which didn't sit well with the 'new' Wagner. Trouble was, Michael's close friendship with Wagner's fiancée meant that he visited their home regularly, even babysitting the kids.

Michael was kind to the children, but in Wagner's twisted mind he was to be suspected nonetheless. Wagner became furious one day when Michael, playing harmlessly with Sally's eldest son, put his hand over the boy's mouth to stop him talking.

The man who had abused Robert Wagner as a child had done the same thing, to keep him quiet.

Michael Gardiner had led a troubled life. His father died when he was young, his mother remarried and Michael's relationship with his stepfather was poor. At fourteen he was placed in foster care after being abused by someone close to him. Desperate to stay away from his foster home, Michael spent his late teens living with his sister or friends. His brother objected to Michael's sexuality and had little to do with him.

Despite his troubled childhood and the prejudices he encountered, friends remember Michael as easygoing. He was warm and friendly.

In late 1997 Michael was boarding with a cousin of Sally Brown named Nicole Zuritta. On 6 September, Zuritta travelled interstate for work and left Michael, nineteen, to look after her house. She returned ten days later to find that her housesitter – and much of her property – had vanished:

> I believed at the time that it could not have been Michael as he didn't drive and he would have needed assistance, just with the amount of stuff taken.
>
> It wasn't until a couple of days later that I thought things were a bit suspicious. I was cleaning out Michael's bedroom when I found his wallet under his bed. The wallet contained Michael's health care card, Medicare card, and a keycard for the Commonwealth Bank.
>
> Near the wallet ... was a letter from Michael. I recognised his handwriting. It was a thank you letter and in it Michael promised to keep in touch.
>
> This made me think that, definitely, something was wrong, along the lines that he had got into the wrong company and they were misguiding him. I didn't think anything bad had happened to him at that time.

★   ★   ★

Weak from his ordeal, Michael Gardiner could barely stand. He had been beaten and tortured but was trying desperately to stay on his feet. He had to. A rope was tied around his neck, with a slipknot at the back. The other end was tied to a beam above him. If Michael did not stand – if he faltered for even a moment – the rope would tighten and he would choke to death.

John Bunting and Robert Wagner were enjoying the spectacle. They laughed out loud as their victim fought to stay alive.

Hours earlier Michael had been abducted from the house he was minding for Nicole Zuritta. Robert Wagner knew he'd been staying there alone.

Michael was taken on the long drive to the house Bunting now occupied in the rural town of Murray Bridge. The victim's horrific final moments came to pass in the garage behind the house. John Bunting later described the killing to James Vlassakis, who told the police:

> He was laughing his head off about how he had murdered Michael. When John Bunting said to Michael to stand up, Michael stood up until basically he couldn't. That was the big joke to John, the fact that he, Michael, tried to stand up . . . and fell down and he died.

During his ordeal Michael had suffered burns to his left arm, as well as his testicles. The burns were later thought to have come from a cigarette pressed against his skin or repeated electric shocks.

★   ★   ★

Before embarking on the murder of Michael Gardiner, Bunting and Wagner developed a plan to explain his disappearance. The first step took place while the victim was still alive; shortly before his death, Michael's captors forced him to make a telephone call. The call was to a family friend with whom Michael was due to move in.

The conversation lasted less than four minutes; Michael sounded tense. In the background his friend could hear voices telling him to 'hurry up and get off the telephone':

> He told me that he was okay and that he did still want to come and live with me but he was going up north to live for a while to sort out some personal problems. I asked him where he was going and he said that he was going to Snowtown. I asked him where he was ringing from but at that time the phone went dead, like it had been cut off . . .

After the killing, Bunting and Wagner looted Nicole Zuritta's home. Since Michael had been housesitting, it would look as though he had stolen the property and then fled.

Next came more phone calls from someone impersonating Michael Gardiner. An answering machine message for Zuritta was among them:

> Nicole, this is Michael, sorry about your stuff but I need the money, don't go to the cops . . .

Zuritta was one of several people told false stories about Michael Gardiner's whereabouts:

Robert said that he and John had seen Michael a day or two earlier at a service station . . .

He said Michael was with some friends, standing near the bowsers talking to someone in a car. Robert also said that he and John had yelled out to Michael 'poofter, thief'. He said that John and he were driving past in a car.

Nicole Zuritta searched the area Wagner had mentioned. She visited the service station, even questioned an employee. Still there was no trace of Michael Gardiner.

FIFTEEN

Thomas Trevilyan was a teenager plagued by acute mental illness and prone to bizarre flights of fancy.

From the age of thirteen he'd been raised by his maternal grandparents, a kind couple who worried for their grandson when he left home a few years later. They would speak to him on the telephone once a week and visit twice a month.

During one such visit in late 1997, Thomas's grandparents encountered a strange, tall man they later learned was Barry Lane. Neighbours told them Lane had been 'hanging around' and they had warned him to stay away.

The next time the couple arrived to see Thomas, he and his possessions were gone. It was another three weeks before he telephoned to say he'd moved house. He told his grandfather he was fine.

Thomas Trevilyan had moved into Barry Lane's rented home in the northeastern suburb of Hectorville. The pair's relationship was almost certainly sexual. It was typical of Lane to prey on a troubled teen to satisfy his own desires.

It was only a matter of time before John Bunting and Robert Wagner turned their murderous attention to Barry Lane. He had served his purpose as Bunting's 'informant'.

In the killers' minds, the time had come for Lane to pay for all he had done.

A convicted paedophile, Lane had lured Robert Wagner at a young age, spiriting the then teenager away from his family and sexually abusing him. Only with the help of John Bunting had Wagner been able to escape Lane's influence.

Now Lane was molesting another young man, Thomas Trevilyan. Bunting and Wagner befriended Thomas and then moved in for the kill.

Barry Lane was murdered on the night of 17 October 1997. He was ambushed in the home he now shared with Trevilyan. Typical of their modus operandi, Bunting and Wagner overpowered Lane and handcuffed him. This time they had Trevilyan's help.

Lane's attackers demanded his bank keycard and personal security number so they could steal his money.

Next, Lane was forced to speak to his mother on the telephone. At the time Sylvia Lane thought the call so strange that she assumed her son was drunk. He unleashed an abusive tirade, telling her he was leaving town and that he planned to hitchhike to Queensland:

> He called me a lot of bad names. He told me he didn't want anything to do with me or the family. I remember that his boyfriend, Thomas, was in the background ... spurring Barry on.

Sylvia was distraught and immediately called her other son, Cyril. After visiting his mother to calm her down, Cyril considered driving to Barry's to demand an explanation, but didn't have enough petrol to make the trip. Cyril's empty fuel tank most likely saved his life.

After the phone call to his mother, it appears that Barry Lane was also forced to speak to his ex-fiancée, Joanna, as she explained to police:

I received a phone call from Barry and Thomas late one evening about ten or eleven o'clock at night. Thomas spoke first and he said that the car was broken down and it would be a couple of days before they could get back. Thomas told me that they were both in Clare, but I didn't believe them because I didn't hear any STD [long distance] pips when I first picked up the phone. Thomas gave the phone to Barry.

Barry told me that they were broken down in Clare and that he would be coming back on Wednesday. He was waiting for his pension cheque to fix the car. Barry, on the phone, asked me to check the mail and to feed the dogs.

The end was near for Lane. A rolled-up bandage was stuffed into his mouth, the gag held in place by yellow duct tape wrapped around his head. More tape was looped under his chin to keep his mouth shut. Bunting and Wagner wanted Lane's screams to be muffled as he was tortured – his toes were crushed with pliers. After he'd been strangled, his body was wrapped in carpet and left in the house. Bunting and Wagner would come back for it later.

A few days after Lane's disappearance his sister, Krystal, who lived in Queensland, received a strange telephone call. The voice was Barry's, but something wasn't quite right:

He said words to the effect 'Oh, it's your brother Barry, I'm coming up, I'll be there in a couple of days. I don't know whether I'll be catching the bus or hitching. Don't tell Mum'.

> I thought it was strange because he didn't say 'It's Barry', like he did every other time he rang me.

Lane's voice was 'strained and edgy'. The telephone was hung up before Krystal had the chance to say anything. She thought at the time that it sounded like a recording.

After Lane's murder Robert Wagner took Thomas Trevilyan under his wing. Others in Wagner's volunteer fire brigade remember Trevilyan tagging along to meetings. He was quiet and never ventured far from Wagner's side.

Trevilyan also moved into the house Wagner shared with Sally Brown and her four children. The new boarder made Sally uncomfortable:

> Robert didn't tell me anything about Thomas when he first moved in. He just said he needed a place to stay. In the first week of Thomas being there, I overheard Thomas and Robert talking about Barry Lane and later John [Bunting] and Robert saying the same things. They were calling him a 'dirty', which is what they called a paedophile. They also spoke of Barry doing the same things to Thomas as he did ... to Robert. I confronted Robert about this and he told me Thomas came from Barry's and he needed a place to stay.

It was at about this time that Thomas Trevilyan visited his cousin, Lenore Penner, and told her the seemingly strange tale of Barry Lane's murder. He confessed how he and two others had killed Barry Lane because he had abused them. He detailed how Lane had been tortured for his banking details, wrapped in plastic bags and tape and then placed in a 44-gallon drum. Thomas said he feared his accomplices would now kill him. It was a story which seemed as outlandish as the many Thomas had told before. Lenore Penner recorded the date in her diary: 30 October 1997.

Not surprisingly, Thomas Trevilyan's mental state – and his behaviour – became even more erratic after Barry Lane's murder. Sally Brown had agreed to let Thomas stay in her home, but she was uncomfortable with his violent outbursts. Upon hearing the slightest noise he would grab a carving knife from the kitchen and run outside. To make matters worse, he wasn't taking his medication.

The final straw came on 4 November 1997, when Thomas threatened one of Sally's daughters:

> He threatened to kill the puppy [she] was holding. [She] was running around the car trying to keep away from him and Thomas was chasing her with a knife in his hand and threatening to cut the dog's throat.
>
> I told Robert he had to get him out of the house. I was frightened of what may have happened. Robert was not impressed but said he would talk to him.
>
> Robert and John took Thomas for a drive that night ... I never saw Thomas again.

There was no reason for the truck driver to glance sideways as he cruised along the road not far from the Adelaide Hills town of Kersbrook, but he did. From his elevated position, the driver glanced down the steep embankment at the side of the road, peering into the bush. There, hanging from a tree, was a young man's body. It was 5 November 1997.

To police the case was seemingly routine. The young man had apparently hanged himself not far from the side of the road. There was still $6.90 in his pocket and a red milk carton at his feet. The body was identified as that of eighteen-year-old Thomas Trevilyan, and local police began compiling a report for the coroner.

An officer telephoned Robert Wagner because Trevilyan had been living with him in the days before his death. Hoping to add to the assumption of suicide, Wagner told the officer that Trevilyan had been suffering mood swings, had threatened to kill the family dog and his behaviour had deteriorated to such a point that Trevilyan was kicked out of the house. Wagner claimed the teenager had returned two days later – 4 November – and threatened to hang himself in the back yard.

In light of what they had seen and heard, investigators declared Thomas Trevilyan's death a suicide.

It remains unclear whether or not Bunting and Wagner knew that Trevilyan had told his cousin about Barry Lane's murder. The pair had most likely considered Trevilyan a risk regardless. Whatever the case, the incident with the knife had prompted them to kill Thomas Trevilyan, and everything had gone exactly according to plan. They had wanted the death to look like a suicide, and police had fallen for the ruse. Bunting was particularly pleased with his final touch: leaving money in one of the teenager's pockets.

Empty pockets, he reasoned, would arouse the suspicions of police.

SIXTEEN

John Bunting's pattern had become clear: he would draw others into his murderous circle, select a victim and kill.

Clinton Trezise had been first, murdered in 1992. Robert Wagner and Barry Lane had helped dispose of the body. From then on, it was Wagner who became Bunting's most willing accomplice – the pair murdering Ray Davies in 1995 and Suzanne Allen a year later.

In late 1997 the killings began to gain momentum. It was late August or early September when Michael Gardiner was killed. Within a month Barry Lane was tortured and murdered, and a few weeks later Thomas Trevilyan was hanged from a tree.

It was Bunting who selected the victims, motivated at first by his hatred of people he deemed were paedophiles. The rage from being abused as children remained. So warped, however, was their view of those around them that only two of their five victims were actually convicted paedophiles: Ray Davies and Barry Lane.

It's likely Trezise and Gardiner were targeted because of their homosexuality – reason enough in the depraved minds of Bunting and Wagner.

Suzanne Allen was killed because her knowledge of Davies's disappearance – combined with her unrequited love for Bunting – made her a risk. Given his erratic behaviour and mental state, Trevilyan too could not be trusted with all that he knew.

By early 1998, any single motive for murder had made way for Bunting and Wagner's greed and bloodlust. And the killers had discovered an unexpected fringe benefit: stealing money from their victims' bank accounts. All the victims had been paid government pensions direct into their accounts, so the cash kept flowing. Bunting – with the help of others – would forge documents, alter bank details, even pose as victims, to ensure the welfare payments were not cut off.

Profit aside, it was the thrill of the kill which Bunting and Wagner craved the most. They loved the power and wanted to feel it again and again. They would label someone a paedophile – in their words, a 'dirty' – not because it was true, but as some kind of justification for killing. It was Bunting who would choose the victims, and his choices were getting much closer to home.

Gavin Porter's life was derailed by his drug addictions. From the age of twenty-three, when his father took him to a health clinic, he had tried to rid himself of the burden. It was a battle he was destined to lose.

Gavin was born in Victoria in 1967 to parents Carol and Trevor. His mother suffered severe depression after the birth and his parents divorced when he was young. It was Gavin's doting grandmother who virtually raised him. He was twenty-four when his mother died of cancer.

A gifted tradesman, Gavin worked as a telephone technician, even spending time working in the Philippines before returning to Australia in 1992. Over the next few years his drug addiction worsened as he travelled to different parts of Australia, drifting from one odd job to the next. By 1994 he was living in South Australia.

Medical records show that, from December 1994, a doctor in Adelaide's western suburbs was prescribing Gavin Porter with methadone. A long-time heroin addict, Porter had been admitted to the methadone program, which meant that, upon visiting a registered pharmacy, he was issued with regular doses of the alternative drug. Health department records list Gavin Porter's last known address, which he gave in early 1998, as 3 Burdekin Avenue, Murray Bridge.

Burdekin Avenue is a nondescript street lined with government-owned housing. It looks like many others in that part of Murray Bridge, a large country centre about an hour and a half's drive east of Adelaide.

By early 1998, 3 Burdekin Ave was home to John Bunting, his de facto wife Elizabeth Harvey, and her four sons – Troy Youde, and James, Adrian and Kristoffer Vlassakis.

Gavin Porter was a friend of Jamie's, and was also living at the house. The pair were both drug addicts on the methadone program and had shared various homes in Adelaide in the past two years. The friends, who had moved in with Jamie's family because they were broke, would spend their days working on Gavin's car and sleeping off the effects of the various drugs they were taking.

John Bunting seemed to pay little attention to the pair, but resented their drug-taking, referring to them as 'waste'.

James Vlassakis can't remember the exact date of Gavin Porter's murder, but it was sometime in the five days after 3 April 1998 – the last day Porter visited his methadone doctor.

In his tell-all interview with police, Vlassakis explained

that on the evening of the killing he had taken his younger brothers to the local drive-in cinema. Vlassakis saw Porter out the front, working on his car, as he left. When he returned home, he was surprised to see that Robert Wagner had come to visit:

> I walked inside, said hello to Mum and that. I remember Robert and John sitting in the lounge and there was Chinese on the table there – on the coffee table . . . I spun out that Robert was up there.

After a brief conversation, Bunting told Vlassakis to come with him to the garage. Wagner followed.

> I can't remember the conversation in the shed, but basically I think we were in there a little bit and John lifted up all these things and showed me Gavin.

Under the old lounge cushions and sheets was the body of Gavin Porter. His knees still raised, he had obvious bruising around his neck where he'd been strangled to death.

James Vlassakis stood terrified as Bunting and Wagner showed them the body of his murdered friend. Bunting had always talked of killing people, incessant ravings which had seen Vlassakis grow fearful of the man he had once seen as a father figure, but never before had Vlassakis been sure that Bunting was capable of murder, that the stories he told were true.

At this moment, Vlassakis knew Bunting was a killer; Wagner too. Vlassakis feared he was to be their next victim – perhaps this was why he'd been brought to the shed and shown his best friend dead on the floor:

> I remember I was pretty scared at the time of seeing this,
> and I remember I looked that he [Bunting] was looking –
> the way he was looking at me. But I can't remember any
> words now. I know he was talking to me.

Later Bunting told Vlassakis the story of Gavin Porter's
murder. How Porter had been asleep in his car when
Bunting and Wagner made their move. How Wagner
looped a rope around Porter's neck and began to strangle
him, Porter fighting back, stabbing Bunting in the hand
with a screwdriver before Bunting leaned on the victim's
chest to squeeze out his final breath.

A few days after the murder Bunting arrived home with
a large, black plastic drum. Again he summoned James
Vlassakis:

> I just remember getting the barrel out of the car and
> going into the shed with it. John uncovered Gavin Porter
> ...moved things around in the shed to make a bit of
> room. There was talking. I can't remember exactly what
> the talk was.
>
> The barrel was laid on the ground ...he was placed in
> there head first. Gavin Porter was put in the barrel and the
> lid was put on.

Bunting then manoeuvred the plastic barrel into a position
alongside another drum. It was almost identical. As he lifted
the lid, Bunting peered inside. 'They're rotting very nicely,'
he said.

The other barrel contained the bodies of Michael
Gardiner and Barry Lane.

True to form, John Bunting had procured another

accomplice: James Vlassakis was now being enlisted into a bizarre group of killers, some of whom had then been killed themselves. He was too scared, perhaps too weak, to do anything but play along.

Vlassakis helped shift Gavin Porter's car to Robert Wagner's house. He accepted Porter's bankcard from Bunting and began stealing his murdered friend's money. Vlassakis – on Bunting's orders – told Porter's friends false stories to explain his disappearance; most were told Porter had moved back to Victoria.

Back in the times when James Vlassakis had trusted, even loved, John Bunting, he had confided in him about the sexual abuse he had endured as a child. One of the people James said had molested him was his older half-brother, Troy Youde.

Youde, also a regular drug user, had never been liked by Bunting. He was now an obvious target. At the time of his murder, between 25 August and 8 September 1998, he was still living in Murray Bridge with his mother, brothers and Bunting.

Youde's was the first of the murders in which James Vlassakis took part. It is also the first for which he later gave police an eyewitness account:

I was – I sleep in the lounge room. I was woken up and handed a club ... Robert Wagner was there and John Bunting was there. I was given the handcuffs, I was given a club, which was a piece off a lounge sofa, and I was taken down to the bedroom where Troy was. As soon as John said 'now', they all started hitting.

Troy stood up, got up, was screaming out ... 'Jamie, what are you doing?' because he seen me there. He jumped on the bed ... jumped on the bed into the wall, backed into the wall. Robert and John just flew in. Troy put his hands up to stop – stop the bats and that. John just kept hitting him, telling him to get down on the floor or something.

John told me 'put the handcuffs on' – not just 'put the handcuffs on' but yelling at me ...

Overwhelmed, Jamie left the room:

As I came back down the hallway, John and Robert were shuffling Troy into the bathroom, which was next door to the bedroom, and they sat him down in the bathtub.

To my understanding he wasn't going to be murdered, he was just going to be bashed and have a bit of a talk-to. John said he wanted to have a talk to him. Then there was – they were in the bathroom and they were talking to him. I think there were a few hits.

John asked him [Troy] to call him 'Lord Sir'. John asked him to call Robert 'God' ... Then he was asked to give me a name. I think Troy said something along the lines of 'Moses' or something. I think it was John or Robert that said that was a Jew's name and then smacked him in the head ... and then he said 'Master'.

Mum was down in Adelaide that day ... Adrian and Kristoffer were with Mum.

John said to Troy – to be good and that he'd let him go, and not to go to the police. He said that he would take him for a drive and drop him off somewhere.

I remember walking down the hallway again sometime ... I couldn't handle it ...

His head bloodied from the repeated blows, Troy Youde

was tortured as he sat handcuffed in the bathtub. John Bunting then Robert Wagner punched him again and again in the testicles; he was told to 'shut up' as he screamed in pain. Wagner crushed one of Troy's toes with pliers – first on the joint, then on the toenail.

Next Bunting produced a small tape recorder, forcing his victim to recite statements into the hand-held device:

> Mum, I can't handle it in this house no more. It's all around me. I'm going to see the earth before there's none left. Wish me luck.
>
> Leave me the fuck alone. I've had enough. Just leave me alone. Everyone just leave me alone.
>
> You're going to stay the fuck out of my life.

Troy was forced to repeat more than twenty sentences, some in an angry, abusive tone directed at his mother and younger brothers. Once his victim was dead Bunting planned to play the recordings, via telephone, to family and friends. This would give the impression that Troy was still alive and had merely run away.

As James Vlassakis watched the tape recordings being made, he realised Bunting wasn't going to let Troy go. His brother would be murdered like all the others. James fled the bathroom, but Bunting called for him to return. It was time, Bunting said, for Troy to apologise.

> So I went in there and kneeled – kneeled down to Troy. I started saying to Troy, 'What you done to me' – the look on Troy's face was, like, fear. Troy said to me that he did say sorry before and he meant it, and he was sorry.

Troy Youde had a sock stuffed in his mouth and silver duct

tape wrapped around his face and head. The bashing continued. As he worked himself into a frenzy, Bunting played music in the background – his favourite album, Live's *Throwing Copper*.

The final act would be Troy's strangulation. Wagner tied blue nylon rope around the victim's neck, leaving a loop at the back. He slid a jack handle into the loop and began twisting. The rope gradually tightened.

> I was looking through the crack of the door and I could see Robert in there doing that with Troy, and then John pulled me into the bathroom. He said, 'No, come in, come in. No, you've got to be here for it.'

During the earlier bashing, however, Wagner had injured his hand and the twisting required too much force.

> . . . it seemed to me that it was taking too long and it was – it was hurting and that. So I grabbed the bar and the rope broke. He started to slouch over towards us, losing consciousness but still conscious. John turned around and said to Troy that this was fun and we could do this all day. Troy sort of looked at John with a – a – a look. I can't explain the look.

Robert Wagner retied the rope and strangled Troy Youde to death as John Bunting kneeled and stared his victim in the eyes.

Once Troy Youde was dead, his body was wrapped in garbage bags and carried to the outside garage. Youde's body was placed in almost the same position Gavin Porter had laid in only a few months before.

Later, Vlassakis listened as his mother and brothers were told false stories to account for Troy's sudden absence:

> Mum returned home that day ... John told Mum that there was a big fight with Troy and that he went and took off; said there was a massive fight between myself, Troy and him.

The following day Bunting and Vlassakis travelled to Adelaide, driving to a northern suburbs scrap yard named Paramount Browns. Bunting purchased a black plastic barrel, similar to the others, for $25.

> John told me I had to help him. Troy was placed into the barrel in a similar way to Gavin Porter, and then John said that the barrel was shorter than the rest – the other two which contained Barry, Michael and Gavin – and he couldn't put both of Troy's feet into the barrel.

John Bunting laughed, even explained his technique, as he used a knife to slice one of the feet from Youde's body.

> Afterwards he [Bunting] said it was my first [murder] and everything like that; asked me how I felt about it – things like that, you know – and I just agreed with him; said to him I enjoyed it. I didn't. Kept the lie going for him because, you know, I thought, well, if he can do that to my brother, he could do it to me.

SEVENTEEN

There was a time when the friendship between John Bunting and Mark Haydon had become strained. Haydon had drifted out of Bunting's posse as Robert Wagner stormed in.

By late 1998, however, Haydon had resumed his place in the group.

Mark Haydon was living in a house in the northern Adelaide suburb of Smithfield Plains which he shared with his wife, Elizabeth, and her two sons. Elizabeth Haydon's sister, Gail Sinclair, and Gail's teenage son, Fred Brooks, were staying in a rumpus room out the back.

John Bunting and Robert Wagner were frequent visitors to the Haydon household. The men would spend hours together, playing computer games, talking and watching TV. Bunting also had another reason to visit: he was having an affair with Gail Sinclair. He would explain his long absences from Murray Bridge by telling his de facto, Elizabeth Harvey, that he'd taken work as a truck driver.

Now back in the fold, Mark Haydon was given an important task. John Bunting, Elizabeth Harvey and her sons were moving out of their Murray Bridge house. They were shifting only a few doors down, but there was nowhere for the bodies in the barrels to be stored.

It was late at night when Bunting and Wagner shifted

the macabre load into a furniture truck and drove to Mark Haydon's house. The remains of Barry Lane, Michael Gardiner, Gavin Porter and Troy Youde, sealed inside three black plastic barrels, were carried into Haydon's garage.

From the day he was born – 7 March 1981 – Fred Brooks was destined to lead a disadvantaged life. Perhaps symbolic of this was the fact that his parents had met in a government welfare office. They had separated while Fred was still a toddler and he spent much of his childhood in foster care.

At fifteen Fred went to live with his father, Fred Brooks senior. Welfare authorities had tracked him down and asked him to give his son a home. Soon afterwards Fred's mother, Gail Sinclair, was back on the scene and the couple reunited. Their son in tow, they travelled through various parts of Australia.

Some two years after it rekindled, the relationship again soured. Fred and his mother set off for Adelaide, moving into a ramshackle rumpus room at the back of a house owned by Gail's sister, Elizabeth Haydon.

Fred's mum found a new boyfriend too: John Bunting.

Fred Brooks dreamed of joining the Air Force, so the seventeen year old enrolled in a local school in the hope of finishing Year 10. He even found a girl he liked, buying her flowers and a necklace for her birthday. They were just friends, though. Later she spoke to police:

> Fred was always friendly, he would never hurt anyone. I
> do know he had a lot of problems. I know he had
> problems with his mum and the guy that was living there
> with his mum [Bunting]. He told me that his mother

treated him like shit; they didn't cook for him or anything like that. He told me that the guy was trying to be like a father to him, but he was not Fred's father and he didn't like him because of that. He was always saying that he wanted to move ...

On the night of Thursday, 17 September 1998, Fred Brooks vanished. He'd returned from a school careers day, excited at his prospects of joining the Air Force, and told his mum he was off to celebrate with his friends.

By the following night, Gail Sinclair began to worry something had happened to her son:

When he hadn't returned by Friday night, I reported him missing. He hadn't used his bank account or anything like that ...

I didn't have a contact number for him. I rang around his friends that I thought he was out with and they said they hadn't seen him, and he hadn't gone out to a party with them, so I panicked and reported him missing.

James Vlassakis was fixing the gearbox in his car when John Bunting called out to him; he had some 'goodies' down the road and needed a hand. Vlassakis assumed the 'goodies' were stolen property, and followed Bunting down the street to the Murray Bridge house they had just moved out of. The place was mostly empty.

At the front door, Bunting paused. He told Vlassakis that Fred Brooks was inside, having been tricked into coming to Murray Bridge. Vlassakis was told to play along.

Brooks was standing with Robert Wagner in the same bedroom where Troy Youde had been taken prisoner. The pair was playing a 'game' with a set of handcuffs, taking it in turns to put them on, then use the key to take them off. Bunting and Vlassakis joined in and a pair of thumbcuffs – which hold a person's hands together by the thumbs – were brought out.

Vlassakis sensed what would happen next:

> The handcuffs were placed on Fred once again, and then the thumbcuffs were placed on him as well, and Robert just grabbed Fred around the neck with his arm. He held him for a while and then John said, 'Let him go, otherwise you'll kill him.' Fred started changing colour in the face, and Robert was squeezing pretty hard.
>
> John was telling Fred to be good, basically, like not to scream, not to yell, not to punch.

James Vlassakis had met Fred Brooks a few times before, always during visits to the Haydon house. Bunting had referred to Fred as a paedophile, a 'dirty', who needed to 'go to the clinic'. Vlassakis suspected that Fred Brooks was not a paedophile – the teenager seemed all right to him. A little slow, but harmless.

John Bunting, however, had made up his mind.

> Fred was then walked or pushed by Robert and John, shuffled into the bathroom. He was told to get into the bath in the same – same way as Troy [Youde] was.

Bunting told Fred Brooks he would be asked 'a few questions'. He was ordered to address Bunting as 'Lord Sir' and Wagner as 'God'. As he lay in the bathtub, restrained by handcuffs and thumbcuffs, the seventeen year old was stripped of his jeans and shirt, and then savagely bashed. There were repeated blows to his groin.

I'm not sure if John grabbed my cigarette or Robert's cigarette, but he stuck a cigarette ... a whole butt up his nose. He also put a cigarette butt, or probably a bit more of a cigarette, into the ear, his right ear. As it was there, John was blowing into the ear to keep the flame hot.

Bunting grabbed a tape recorder and, as he had done during the torture of Troy Youde, forced his victim to recite statements directed at his mother and other family and friends. Again Bunting planned to play them to people on the telephone, to give the impression that Fred had vanished of his own free will.

As Bunting delivered a line, it was repeated by Fred:

Hi Mum, it's me, Fred. I'm on me way to Perth. I've met a pretty nice chick. I will be back some time after Christmas.

Yeah Mum, you're just a user, you just want my money. I don't want to see you again. I'm going to Perth. Bye.

I'm fine. I don't know why you're fucking ringing me. Fuck off and leave me the fuck alone.

Bunting quizzed him about banking details and wrote down his answers.

As Wagner crushed one of the victim's toes with pliers, John Bunting set up his latest torture device. The 'Variac' was an electrical apparatus, designed for use in metallic electroplating. Once it is plugged into mains power, a current flows along the Variac's cable, then out through two metal alligator clips. A circular dial controls the amount of electricity released – anything between 0 and 260 volts.

As Bunting explained the workings of the Variac to a terrified Fred Brooks, the alligator clips were attached to his body – one to his penis, the other to one of his testicles. The first shock was at about 20 volts.

Fred started to shake in the bathtub, clenched – the pain – he didn't actually scream or anything but you could tell ...

As he was tortured with repeated electric shocks, Fred was questioned about a girl Bunting believed he had molested. The molestation was almost certainly a figment of Bunting's imagination – justification for his latest kill.

John Bunting was asking him questions about being a dirty – Did he touch the girl? What did he do? – Fred was denying it. He said it never happened, it's not true ... and that's when John did torture on him.

Eventually, John asked him after a while and he said to John that he did. To me it just looked like – Fred was just saying that it happened to stop [the torture].

John often listened to the cassette afterwards and you could – as it played you could hear John asking Fred something and you could hear a punch from Robert into Fred, because Robert punched Fred while the cassette was being made, and after that John loved playing it.

Fred's ordeal was far from over. He suffered cigarette lighter burns at the hands of Robert Wagner, who then produced party-style sparklers. Wagner pulled one of the wire sparklers from its packet, driving it down the eye of the victim's exposed penis, and then igniting the top. It burned down into Fred's flesh and the horrific act was repeated once more.

Further electric shocks were administered by Bunting. Fred was told not to scream, and complied until it was no longer possible, at which point a stocking was stuffed into his mouth and tape wrapped around his head.

The final act of barbarity perpetrated on Fred Brooks was having water injected into various parts of his groin and legs. Like everything else they had done to the helpless teenager, Bunting and Wagner delighted in this.

It's unclear how long the abuse lasted before the end finally came for Fred Brooks. It's also unclear exactly how he died, although the medical evidence suggests he asphyxiated on his gag. For his part, James Vlassakis can't recall:

> I remember seeing Fred on the floor, wrapped up in garbage bags with his knees in the air. I remember cleaning up the bathroom with John ... the sparklers, I think there were gloves ... His clothes that he was wearing were put into garbage bags.

Bunting kept Fred Brooks's identification, bankcard and mobile telephone. His body was carried to the boot of an old car in the back yard. The car was eventually towed away by Mark Haydon and Fred's body dumped on the floor of Haydon's garage until another barrel was bought.

In the days after Fred Brooks's murder, a series of events orchestrated by John Bunting created the impression that Fred had run away. The first was when Bunting and Mark Haydon returned from a trucking job, telling the boy's concerned mother they had seen him at a local service station. They claimed Fred had been in a car with a woman, and that he'd been aggressive, and 'off his face' on speed.

Gail had also called her son's mobile telephone, only to be greeted with a strange, abusive message. It was his voice but it seemed out of character.

Three days after Fred vanished, there was a telephone call to the Haydon household. Elizabeth answered the phone; she recognised Fred's voice as she listened to the barrage of abuse.

After consulting Fred's mum, Elizabeth called the local police station, telling an officer the teenager was no longer missing. It appeared he'd left home of his own free will. Having been opened only nine days before, the police missing persons file for Fred Brooks was marked 'no longer active'.

EIGHTEEN

John Bunting's urge to kill had become overwhelming. It had been only weeks since the last murder and he was again searching for prey. He was cruising the streets of Murray Bridge when he spotted the next victim. James Vlassakis was with him:

Myself and John Bunting, we'd be driving around Murray Bridge, either up to Woolworths [supermarket] or to the main street to do other things. We would see Gary O'Dwyer walking down the road all the time. He was always walking everywhere, and John would make comments about Gary – how he looked like Troy [Youde].

He would say to me ... 'Look at that fag – you know he looks so much like Troy.'

I didn't really want to have a bar of it, but when you're in that situation with John, you had to play his game. We never actually met [Gary] or anything like that. This went on for ... I think all the time I was up at Murray Bridge.

Gary O'Dwyer lived next door to friends of Vlassakis, which is how they came to finally meet:

I think I was coming out to my car and going, and he started talking to me over the fence, and asked me my name and how I was and things like that. He came across as very slow to me ... that's what I would say because of the way he spoke.

John asked me to introduce myself to Gary, and get to know him a little and – and see what he was on, like a pension, and see if he had a family or anything like that. If John asked me to do something, I would.

Gary O'Dwyer was eighteen months old, holding his own bottle and sitting on the counter at the child welfare office when Maureen Fox first laid eyes on him. In 1971 this abandoned baby boy became the ninth foster child taken in by Maureen and her husband, Dalmain. Others had not wanted Gary because he was epileptic and small for his age. This kind couple not only gave Gary a home but intended to adopt him. However, when Maureen's husband died suddenly in 1974 it was no longer possible.

Despite the setback, Maureen considered Gary to be her son and raised him at the same time as one other foster son and five foster daughters. Gary was closest to Debbie and Denise. The family lived in the Adelaide Hills, initially on a farm.

As one of his foster sisters would later describe him, Gary was a 'lost soul' – a loner. Despite the love of his family, he began to lead a nomadic existence from the age of fifteen, sometimes living on the streets and becoming embroiled in petty crime. Once caught, he was always honest with police; Gary had never been much of a liar.

On Christmas Day 1994, Gary O'Dwyer was struck by a hit-and-run driver as he walked along a main road south of Adelaide. Left for dead, he lay on the side of the road until noticed by a truck driver the following morning. Unconscious for a week, Gary had steel plates inserted into his shattered skull and left leg. After six months of rehabilitation, it was clear that he would never make a full recovery. Brain damage resulted in memory loss and an inability to perform basic functions such as arithmetic. He walked with a permanent limp.

By 1997 Gary had moved into a rented house in the town of Murray Bridge. His only income was a disability pension paid by the government, although he received a compensation payout as a result of the accident. In part due to the lasting effects of his injuries, Gary became a heavy drinker and drug user. His petty crime continued – often out of need rather than greed – and he struggled to control his temper. More than once an angry outburst landed him in further trouble with the law.

Another of Gary's weaknesses was his trusting nature. Loneliness made him quick to befriend others, sometimes strangers, and just as quick to trust them. There were occasions when Gary would give a new 'friend' the key to his home, then return to find he'd been robbed.

It was 26 October 1998 when Maureen Fox last saw her foster son. He was twenty-nine years old:

He was walking down Swanport Road [Murray Bridge]. He was dressed in black pants and a black jumper, he had been shopping and was carrying it over his right shoulder . . . walking back towards his home.

I couldn't stop to speak to him. I never saw or heard from him after that date.

Within weeks of that final sighting Maureen Fox spent time in hospital, too unwell to check on Gary. At one point there was a call from Gary's lawyer asking where he was, although he didn't say why.

Maureen was worried about her troubled foster son, but it never occurred to her to report him missing:

> I didn't want to be seen as the interfering mother and considered that Gary was capable of looking after himself and would contact me in his own due time. I never thought anything sinister had happened to Gary.

James Vlassakis was driving along a Murray Bridge street as he saw John Bunting's car approaching. The lights flashed, so he stopped. As Bunting wound down his window, Vlassakis could see Robert Wagner in the passenger seat.

Bunting quizzed Vlassakis on his plans for the night, and then told him to 'put off' the party to which he was headed.

> He said something like, 'What about Gary [O'Dwyer], can we do Gary? Tell him you've got a couple of friends that want to come for a drink. We'll go up to the pub now and grab some drinks and we'll meet you ...'

Vlassakis had no trouble selling the idea to Gary O'Dwyer when he called him:

> I said to John, 'That's fine, you can go around there, and I'm going ... I'm going to this party now.' John turned around and said, 'No, no. You get in this car and you can go after.'

It was nightfall as the trio walked into Gary O'Dwyer's home. Vlassakis introduced Gary to John Bunting and Robert Wagner:

I was just sitting there, pretty quiet, because I knew what was going to happen. Gary got up, got a few glasses and that. John turned around to me and said, 'Well I've got to get him a bit pissed' ... and asked me if I could skol a few drinks with Gary.

There was a Mississippi Moonshine, bottle of that. John poured the two glasses – mine and Gary's – pretty much full to the top.

I think we were talking for about ten, maybe fifteen, maybe twenty minutes. It wasn't that long really at all. Gary got up to show Robert something and John also stood up, and then Robert just grabbed Gary around the throat.

A small man, Gary O'Dwyer was no match for the height and strength of Robert Wagner.

John said to Robert to like, 'Ease off a bit. Let him go, otherwise you'll kill him', because Gary ... went into some sort of fit as soon as Robert grabbed him ... and then Robert released him and he sort of half fell down and then started to get back up. He was, like, getting in breaths of air, looking, trying to work out what's going on – asking, 'What's going on? What are you doing? What's this for?'

John was telling him to shut up – 'Speak when I speak to you.'

Robert or John put handcuffs on, I can't remember who did it now. He [O'Dwyer] was taken into the kitchen where a mattress was standing up against the wall. He was made to sit down on the mattress.

He wasn't resisting them. He was in shock, like he was panicking, you know, shaking in his hands and that ... when he was sitting on the mattress his legs were shaking.

They started talking to him, asking him if he was a dirty – things like that – and saying he was a dirty. He said no, he wasn't, and Robert clobbered him one in the head, just with a fist. He started screaming.

Like others before him, Gary was told to address Bunting as 'Lord Sir' and Wagner as 'God'. When he got the names wrong, he was beaten.

Vlassakis was sent to Bunting's car, returning with the Variac machine and a plastic bag packed with other items:

Robert Wagner started pulling things out of the bag and there was the sparklers ... lighters ... there was tape and things like that.

John grabbed the Variac and then said – 'you didn't grab the leads' – I went back to the car to grab those leads. All the leads for the Variac – the clamps, the leads.

Wagner was next to Gary as Bunting sat at the kitchen table asking their victim a series of questions about his banking details, pension and family background. If Gary was slow to answer, he would be hit by Wagner.

John Bunting used the Variac. He sat down – kneeled down in front of Gary – so he was like, looking at Gary at head height, and then he was explaining to Gary how the Variac worked. And I think that's when Robert pulled off Gary's jeans ... and then it was connected up.

John Bunting attached two clamps to Gary – I remember one being on his testicles – and I can't remember what number [voltage] he went up to but Gary was violently jumping around on the mattress.

It was a sickening routine James Vlassakis had witnessed –
and taken part in – twice before. This time he could not
stand to stay. He used his friend's party as his excuse:

> I think that's when I said to John that I had to go ...
> people would come looking for me and I had to go.
>
> I'd seen enough before; I didn't want to be there.
>
> John accepted that, so again to make my position
> better, I walked over to Gary and I started hitting him in
> the – in the chest, I think about four or five times.

As best Vlassakis can recall, it was somewhere around nine
o'clock at night when he walked out the door, leaving
Gary O'Dwyer to die at the hands of Bunting and
Wagner.

The day after Gary O'Dwyer's murder, John Bunting again
enlisted the help of James Vlassakis. The pair returned to
loot the victim's house.

It was a risky visit, because Gary's neighbours, Kim and
Steven, also knew Vlassakis. They would surely be suspicious
if they saw what was happening. However, John Bunting
had already come up with a plan. Kim recalls the knock at
her door:

> Steven and I were at home ... when John Bunting and
> James Vlassakis pulled into Gary's driveway. There was a
> trailer attached to the rear of the car.
>
> John and Jamie came to our front door ... both told us
> Gary had moved to Sydney because [people] had bashed
> him up.
>
> They told us they had bought all the furniture from
> Gary for $200. John told us that he had the keys and they

were going in to get the furniture; whilst he was telling us this, I saw the keys in his hand.

They told Steven and I to come into the house and have a look around, because if there was any furniture they didn't want . . . we could have it.

In the kitchen I could smell a bad smell coming from the laundry. I didn't go into the laundry, but when I mentioned something about the smell, John or Jamie told me that Gary had taken the meat out of the freezer and put it into the laundry sink, and it was that meat that was smelling as though it was rotting.

It's unclear whether Gary O'Dwyer's body was still in the laundry when the neighbours were taken into his house. Within days of the murder, his remains became part of the gruesome collection contained in barrels in Mark Haydon's garage.

NINETEEN

John Bunting was mates with Mark Haydon, but he had always despised Haydon's wife, Elizabeth. Behind the couple's back Bunting spoke openly of this hatred, referring to her as 'disgusting', and a 'dirty bitch'.

It's unclear exactly why Bunting finally chose to murder Elizabeth Haydon – perhaps because of his repulsion or his urge to kill again.

There was also the likelihood that Elizabeth Haydon knew too much. It's possible she had become curious about the barrels stored in her garage and the foul smell emerging from them.

There was also the fact that Mark Haydon had revealed details of the first murder to his wife, relaying information John Bunting had told him about how Clinton Trezise – whom Bunting dubbed 'Happy Pants' – had been dumped in a paddock. The revelation had angered Bunting, who conveyed his feelings to James Vlassakis:

> He did say to me that Mark had told [Elizabeth] about Happy Pants being murdered and how Happy Pants was taken to ... Lower Light and buried. John said she knew too much. [She] told John of what she knew ... and how Mark told her.
>
> John said to me ... that Mark had a big mouth.

Whatever the motive, John Bunting had decided it was time for Elizabeth Haydon to die. The night of her murder was sometime between 20 and 26 November 1998 – almost certainly Saturday the 21st. With Mark Haydon and Gail Sinclair out of the house, Bunting and Wagner were free to begin their murderous routine.

There is no eyewitness account of this killing, but the evidence suggests that Elizabeth Haydon's death was as horrific and brutal as those before her. Afterwards Bunting would joke among his group about how Elizabeth had at first thought being taken captive was some kind of joke.

Like the other victims, she was overpowered and handcuffed. Elizabeth was led to her own bathroom and forced to sit in the bathtub. What occurred next was undoubtedly a barrage of beatings and torture.

Death came in the form of asphyxiation. A sock had been stuffed into her mouth, forcing back her tongue, and tape wrapped around her head. A rope, fashioned into a noose, was slipped around her neck.

Once the deed was done, Elizabeth's body was carried to her garage and placed into a barrel which stood alongside four others.

While his wife was being murdered, Mark Haydon had taken her sister for 'a drive' into Adelaide's southern suburbs. The trip had been prompted by a series of false stories concocted by John Bunting.

Gail Sinclair would later detail for police the events of that night:

> We drove home, we got onto Port Wakefield Road and pulled into a service station … and he [Mark] said, 'I'll ring home and let them known we're not far away'. He

came back to the car and said, 'All hell's broke loose at home'.

When the pair arrived home, Bunting claimed Elizabeth had made a pass at him, sparking a fight. She was in her room, upset, and should be left alone. Gail went with Bunting to get some dinner, and when they returned Mark Haydon claimed his angry wife had gone out with 'a boyfriend'.

The following day Haydon reported that his wife had come home in the early hours, drunk, and then run off with her boyfriend for good. To Gail Sinclair, it sounded plausible:

> To me it didn't seem really a lot out of the ordinary because there were times when she was prone to keeping a boyfriend secret and disappearing from the ex [former partner]. Like when she left Ian ... her husband at the time, when she left him she kept the guy that she was seeing secret and just disappeared.
>
> So it didn't seem out of the ordinary to me at the time, but the longer she was gone without any contact with the family [it] didn't seem to sit right. But everyone was saying to me that, you know, she didn't want any contact ... and she wouldn't contact me because I was in the same house as Mark.

Elizabeth's brother was not so convinced. That weekend Garion Sinclair had been babysitting Elizabeth's two boys, William and Christopher. They were the only two of her seven children still in her care, but Elizabeth often unloaded them onto family.

On the Sunday evening, 22 November, Mark came alone to collect the boys. He explained that Elizabeth was at home sleeping.

The next morning, however, the children arrived back on Garion's doorstep. Upset, they had walked there after Mark dropped them at school. The boys said their mother wasn't at home and they didn't want to stay. Worried, Garion kept William and Christopher with him, setting off to seek advice from child welfare authorities:

> On our return ... Mark was there. The boys did not want to speak to Mark, so I sent them inside whilst I spoke to Mark out the front near his car.
>
> I asked him why [Elizabeth] was not at home on Sunday. He said [she] had come home drunk at about 4.30 a.m. on Sunday morning. She apparently slept it off, and on waking later that morning, she packed a few bags of clothing and then telephoned her boyfriend to come pick her up.
>
> I asked Mark why he did not try to stop her and he replied that her boyfriend had brought his friends with him and that he could not do anything about it.
>
> I thought it was strange [Elizabeth] had a boyfriend, considering the fact [she] never went anywhere without Mark. He also said [she] had cleared his bank account out, along with his father's.

Garion suggested to Mark Haydon he should report Elizabeth missing, and tell police about the stolen money. He refused.

The following night Garion called round to see if his sister had come home. Finding she was still not there, he waited until morning to report Elizabeth missing to police. It was 25 November.

As time passed Garion became increasingly suspicious of his brother-in-law. His concerns heightened when, a week after the disappearance, Mark Haydon inexplicably changed his story:

Mark said [Elizabeth] had accused him of sleeping with Gail. They had an argument about the allegation and he had denied it. He said he had gone out to see his father at the nursing home ... when he came home, she was gone.

There was no mention of [her] alleged boyfriend from Mark's earlier version.

Haydon also paid a bizarre visit to Elizabeth's mother, as she told police:

Mark turned up at my house, he sat on my lounge and the only thing he said was, 'She's gone.' He couldn't look at me; he just couldn't look at me. He then stood up and walked out. He didn't say anything else. I have no idea why he came around, that is all he told me. He was at my house for about five minutes – that was the last time I saw Mark.

The missing persons file tagged 'Elizabeth Haydon' landed on Detective Greg Stone's desk the day after the report was made. The senior constable, based in the northern suburbs, wasted no time beginning his investigations. He was on a late shift, so it was about eleven o'clock at night when he knocked on Mark Haydon's door. From the start Stone thought it odd that Haydon hadn't been the one to report his wife missing.

There was a brief conversation, after which Haydon and Gail Sinclair agreed to visit the police station that night to give statements about Elizabeth's disappearance.

Inside the police complex Mark Haydon was handed a pen and paper. He was asked to record his version of events in writing; the last time he'd seen his wife, where he believed she was. In the space of one and a half messy, error-ridden pages, Haydon wrote about taking Gail for a drive, returning to find his wife had made a pass at John Bunting. Robert Wagner had been there as well. Haydon claimed he fought with his wife that night, then she went out with a 'boyfriend', only to return drunk. The next day the couple apparently clashed again. Haydon said he left and, on his return, his wife was gone. Their marriage was over.

At the same time, in a nearby room, Gail Sinclair was interviewed about her sister's last known movements. She told a similar story, her answers recorded on video and audio cassettes. The interview finished at 12.20 a.m.

Next to be questioned were John Bunting and Robert Wagner. In a written statement, Bunting claimed Elizabeth had tried to kiss him while her husband and sister were out of the house. She became angry when he spurned her advance, then sulked in her bedroom. Bunting said Robert Wagner had walked in on the incident. Wagner's version of events was the same.

Detective Stone, however, suspected murder and began to apply pressure to his suspects. Over the next few weeks, Mark Haydon's home was repeatedly searched. During one search, under a pile of clothes, Detective Stone discovered Elizabeth's purse, documents and bankcards still inside.

On another occasion Elizabeth's gold wedding band and diamond engagement ring, which she always wore, were found in a dressing table drawer. Some of her soiled clothes were found in a garbage bag.

Expert crime scene officers were called in to examine Haydon's home. Using Luminol spray – which highlights traces of blood under ultra-violet light – they detected a small blood stain on the laundry wall. Mark Haydon and Gail Sinclair said it was from one of their dogs, which had given birth to pups in the laundry. A sample was taken nonetheless.

Also searched was Haydon's garage. In the pit – designed for working under cars – officers noted a foul odour and what appeared to be insect casings. Unbeknownst to the detectives, it was the same place where the bodies in the barrels had stood only days – perhaps only hours – before.

TWENTY

It is a trait of most serial killers to keep 'trophies' from each of their crimes. For John Bunting, these trophies were the victims' bodies. While his earliest victims had been buried – and Trevilyan hanged to look like a suicide – the others were kept in large plastic drums. Occasionally Bunting would peer into each barrel, remarking about how well the contents were rotting, sometimes reliving the murder of that particular victim.

Bunting's barrel collection began while he was living at Murray Bridge. Eventually the bodies of Michael Gardiner, Barry Lane, Gavin Porter and Troy Youde came to be stored there.

Bunting had no sense of smell, so he did not notice the pungent odour created by the decomposing remains. He would regularly ask Vlassakis how bad the smell was, and use air fresheners in a bid to disguise it. Some visitors to the house noticed the stench regardless:

> In the back garden they had a shed big enough to fit a car in. It really smelt around the back of the shed. It smelt like dead cats. It smelt like rotting flesh, like what you smell when you see a dead cat on the side of the road.

When Bunting, Elizabeth Harvey and her sons moved out of the house, the landlord too noticed something on the nose:

> I do remember, on returning to the premises ... detecting a horrible smell, which smelt like a rotting and decaying sheep. It was a smell similar to rotting meat. I only say sheep because for years [we] lived on a farm where we had smelt rotting sheep in the paddocks.

The landlord also spotted strange dark stains on the garage's cement floor. They appeared to be circular in shape.

Bunting and Wagner used a truck to shift the barrels from Murray Bridge. They were destined for the garage at Mark Haydon's house, in the northern Adelaide suburb of Smithfield Plains. James Vlassakis recalls coming home late at night, stumbling across the move:

> As I walked up the driveway, John and Robert were actually in the truck ... they were tying the barrels into the truck at that stage. I sat there, had a bit of a conversation with John, and in that conversation he told me that they were going to Mark's place.

When John Bunting realised Elizabeth Haydon had been reported missing, he was enraged – and he panicked. It was only a matter of time, he assumed, before the police would want to search Mark Haydon's house, and that meant the barrels in his garage would have to be shifted – and fast.

By this time, late November 1998, there were five barrels containing seven victims: Michael Gardiner, Barry Lane, Gavin Porter, Troy Youde, Fred Brooks, Gary O'Dwyer and Elizabeth Haydon.

Bunting decided that the best way to transport the barrels would be in the old Toyota Land Cruiser sitting in Mark Haydon's yard. Gail Sinclair was told to stay inside and keep watch for the police while the barrels were being moved:

> John turned up that night and they seemed pretty edgy for some reason and I couldn't figure it out. I thought ... they might have had stolen property or something on the premises.
>
> They just said they had to get – get stuff that would get them arrested if the cops did a search of the house.
>
> They had stuff they had to move, right, and they got me to stay in the family room and keep an eye out in case the police came back or something. And they reversed the Land Cruiser ... through the gates and towards the shed. And they took some stuff out of the manhole in the house and they got a whole heap of old blankets and wrapped stuff in old blankets and put that into the Land Cruiser.
>
> It would have been midnight till three in the morning.
>
> John went and got the trailer while they [the others] were doing something, and then he came back with the trailer, and they put the Land Cruiser onto the trailer and took it away, right. They used Robert's car to tow the trailer away.

The Land Cruiser had to be towed because it was unregistered and might have attracted police attention on the road. The old four-wheel drive's destination was a property in the small rural district of Hoyleton, almost two hours north of Adelaide.

Friends of Bunting rented the property and they had agreed to let him store the vehicle there. Bunting telephoned at ten o'clock that night, but it was in the early hours of the morning when Kathy Jones★ peered out her window to see that Bunting – and Robert Wagner – had arrived. She followed her husband, Simon, outside.

I immediately smelt a foul smell. It smelt like a really bad rotting meat smell. I saw John's [Bunting's] blue Ford Marquis in the driveway with a car trailer attached to the rear. There was a khaki-coloured Toyota four-wheel drive parked behind the car trailer with the … winch still attached.

I saw Robert Wagner unhook the winch from the Toyota whilst John Bunting and Simon stood nearby.

I asked John whether the Toyota was stolen and he said it wasn't. I believed him because there were number plates still attached to it. On asking what the smell came from, John told me it was kangaroo carcasses. He mentioned the kangaroo carcasses were in the drums. I said he could leave the Toyota there, but he had to put it at the southwestern corner of the block so that the smell didn't bother me.

A couple of days later I was outside checking on the lambs when I tried to approach the Toyota four-wheel drive. As I walked towards it I smelt the foul odour again. I was not able to get closer than about 20 feet … because of the smell coming from it. It was then that I noticed there was what appeared to be sheets and blankets over the windows.

John continued to come up to my place about every two weeks. Sometimes Robert Wagner … I think it was the first visit since dropping the Toyota off that John spoke about kangaroo shooting. He mentioned that Robert … and himself had this little business going where they shot kangaroos, minced the meat up and sold it for pet food. The remaining carcass was what he had then placed in the barrels he had stored in the Toyota. I suggested he empty the carcasses down the creek where, if someone else saw them, it wouldn't appear unusual on a sheep station.

Bunting claimed he could not dump the carcasses, because they had been shot with unregistered guns, and they could be traced back.

Several times Kathy Jones telephoned Bunting to complain about the stink the 'kangaroos' were creating. He made repeated promises to move the four-wheel drive, but never did.

When Simon, Kathy and their children moved to a rented house in nearby Snowtown in January 1999, Bunting and Wagner helped them. The four-wheel drive moved too – into the family's driveway. And if the wind blew in the wrong direction, the stench would drift into the house.

At this point, four barrels were locked inside the vehicle. The killers hadn't been able to squeeze in the fifth, as they hurredly shifted evidence from Mark Haydon's home. The final barrel was taken elsewhere: stashed in an old car in the back yard of James Vlassakis's Murray Bridge home.

It was not until John Bunting found a new hiding place that all five of his 'trophies' were again stored together.

Snowtown's former State Bank building was a reminder of the town's demise. The plain red-brick structure once housed a thriving branch. In its day it had been the hub of a burgeoning farming community.

When times on the farms got tough and the rot set into Snowtown, the branch was doomed. In August 1995 bank staff closed the doors for the last time. Four months later the building was sold for a mere $43 000. Its buyers, local farming couple Andrew and Rosemary Michael, believed the building's prime location would make it a sound investment.

It was a secure building with large metal front doors. Inside there was a kitchen, toilet, manager's office and customer counter. In the centre of the building was a strongroom – the vault – with a thick steel door and an old-fashioned combination-and-key lock. Attached to the bank building, but with no internal access, was a small residence which had been the bank manager's home.

An elderly local woman leased the building from the Michaels and was living in the residence while running a plant shop from the main building. Within a year or so the shop's popularity waned; the old woman stayed in the house but the Michaels were forced to find new tenants for the main building.

In January 1999 the Michaels received a call from a man named John. He wanted to rent the bank, and met with Rosemary Michael the next day, as she later recalled:

He was waiting outside the bank in a small white station wagon and was with another man whom he introduced to me as Mark. Neither of them gave their surnames. I showed John through the old bank. John did all the talking and I think Mark hardly said anything at all. John told me that he needed to store equipment, that they made . . . alloy parts for old motorbikes and cars.

John also asked me for a key to the vault. We agreed that I would leave the key in the bank for John . . . [he] mentioned that he wouldn't have to worry about a key as he had a friend who was a locksmith and he'd be able to work it out.

Bunting agreed to rent the building for sixty dollars a week. He paid two weeks' rent in advance, along with a cash bond. The rental agreement listed the names John Bunting and Mark Lawrence (Haydon's former surname).

On 8 February, Rosemary Michael called in at the bank building. Nothing appeared to have been moved in, although the vault door was now locked:

> A few days later John rang me and said that his locksmith mate had locked the vault and that he had stored all he had to in there.

For the most part the new tenants paid their rent on time and hardly ever seemed to visit. The men attracted little attention; their comings and goings at odd hours only occasionally stirred the old lady next door.

Once the lease for the old bank had been signed, the barrels were moved into the vault. Bunting, Wagner and Mark Haydon arrived at Kathy and Simon's house after dark, a trailer attached to Haydon's car.

'We've come to move the happy roos,' Bunting joked.

Not long after that, Simon Jones, who repaired computers and electrical equipment, asked if he could use the bank's foyer as a storage area. Bunting agreed, as Simon recounted to police:

> The first time that I had gone over to the bank with John and Robert after the barrels had been put in the vault, I saw Robert open the door. There was a strong smell coming from inside, which smelt like rotting meat, and I saw Robert go inside to check the drums. When Robert

came out of the vault, he said to John that the roos weren't happy and that they were very smelly. They both found that very funny.

At some stage after this, I went into the bank to check the letterbox; it was on this occasion that I could smell the rotting meat coming from the vault. The next time John rang me or came to see me, I told him the smell was getting into the bank. The next time I went to check the mail, I opened the door of the vault and noticed that black plastic had been stuck in the doorway.

The first James Vlassakis learned of the old bank at Snowtown was in April 1999. On Bunting's orders he had gone there with Mark Haydon to fetch the rent book and then pay the rent at the local post office.

When the pair went inside the bank the vault was locked, and they could see nothing untoward.

Vlassakis's next visit – about a week later – will be etched in his mind forever:

> It was John Bunting, Robert Wagner, myself and Mark Haydon. We all went up to the bank, but before we went up to the bank, we went to Robert's place. I was told to take a change of clothes, Robert was told – by John Bunting – to take a change of clothes, same as Mark Haydon.

The men loaded buckets, hoses and bags of pre-mix cement into Mark Haydon's car, then set off. On the way, James Vlassakis worried he was being taken there to die:

> They knew I was shitting myself, absolutely shitting myself, because I thought I was going to be knocked that night for sure – to the point where I was shaking in the car and

everything like that, and the conversations, I can't specifically remember the conversations but they were about other – the other previous murders and stuff like that.

We walked into the bank. I think John asked us about the smell – if it smelt really bad. I think that's when John placed an air freshener in the bank and went into the vault. John manipulated the lock and then we entered the vault itself. John and Robert were lifting the lids off all the barrels and having a look in there. [There was] liquid in the barrels and they were worse than . . . before.

John had a look – I think it was [Elizabeth Haydon's] barrel – said something along the lines that he couldn't believe how quick she was rotting – then just went along to all the others and eventually went into . . . Troy's barrel and he said something about Troy. There was a lot of laughing by John and Robert.

They opened up the two doors to the bank; the front main doors – dropped the tailgate of Mark's [car] and unloaded the car – the concrete, buckets, hoses. I think there was a white shopping bag full of stuff and that was all thrown into the bank.

John then said that he was going to cut the bodies up so they were smaller and then he was going to put concrete into the bottom of the barrels. He . . . wanted to put them in a boat and then take them out to sea and just dump them in the sea.

After everything was unloaded, he went into the bank vault again. When the main doors were open the vault was closed, and then it was reopened again when those doors were closed and the place was locked up, so we were locked inside.

He [Bunting] – and Robert Wagner – started cutting up Troy. They had two barrels opened. One was where

Troy was and then there was another one open. They chopped off [Troy's] legs and that. Robert cut off all the . . . muscles and that so it was down to the bone, and threw that into the other barrel.

During the process . . . I walked out of the actual vault. I couldn't handle that, and Mark was outside . . . having a cigarette. I had a cigarette myself. I was smoking like a train through nerves, fear, and Mark said something like he couldn't handle it . . . he couldn't stomach it. It was too gruesome.

[I] stayed out of the vault for a while, and then entered the vault again, just to see how long John was going to be. He said . . . Troy's balls . . . they were filthy. I can't remember the exact words. He cut them off, or started cutting down there, and then just started stabbing with a knife.

After mutilating Troy Youde's body, Bunting and Wagner put the lids back on the open barrels and locked the vault. It was getting late; their work would have to be continued another time.

The four men walked across the nearby rail line to Kathy and Simon Jones's house. Vlassakis couldn't wait to scrub himself clean:

I went and had a shower at Simon and Kathy's . . . my clothes reeked; my hair. I was only in the vault for – I don't know how long but it wasn't a long time – the stench just got into me.

For their part, Kathy and Simon Jones didn't think it odd that their friends had come for a shower. They assumed they'd been over at the bank, working on the 'kangaroo' carcasses.

TWENTY-ONE

The police investigation had begun in July 1997, as a routine review of a missing persons case: Clinton Trezise. Four months later Barry Lane, another missing person, had been linked to the inquiry. At first there was nothing to suggest foul play and certainly no evidence of murder.

It was not until July 1998 that Robert Wagner was filmed by a hidden camera, stealing money from Barry Lane's bank account. Even then it was proof of nothing more than theft, or perhaps fraud. The case was still considered a low priority.

Surveillance, and the specially trained officers needed to follow the target, were particularly difficult to access. In the six months after being filmed by the security camera, Robert Wagner was physically tagged on less than half a dozen occasions. Keen for more resources to be devoted to his investigation, Detective Craig Patterson even sought the help of a Federal Police surveillance team.

Telephone intercepts, too, were a problem. Patterson first made an intercept application in October 1998, but SA Police had only six intercept lines, and none was available.

It was not until Elizabeth Haydon vanished that the inquiry significantly intensified. The disappearances of Suzanne Allen and Ray Davies were also linked to the case and a major police operation began. By January 1999 the telephone intercept lines were made available and the rate of physical surveillance increased – but it was still not daily.

It is a tragedy that in the course of sixteen months, while police inquiries were under way, the killers were able to claim eight victims: Michael Gardiner, Barry Lane, Thomas Trevilyan, Gavin Porter, Troy Youde, Fred Brooks, Gary O'Dwyer and Elizabeth Haydon.

However, even with the power of hindsight, it is difficult to see how these deaths could have been prevented. During this time, police had uncovered nothing to suggest that such horrific crimes were occurring. Most of the victims – because of their isolation or the false impressions created by the killers – had not been reported missing.

David Johnson's murder, however, occurred during the intense phase of the police investigation.

By this point, there was a reasonable suspicion of murder. John Bunting, Robert Wagner and Mark Haydon had been identified as suspects in the deaths of four missing persons – Clinton Trezise, Suzanne Allen, Barry Lane and Elizabeth Haydon. Their disappearances had been declared major crimes.

Despite all this, the suspects were still not subject to daily surveillance. Between 25 February and 20 May 1999, the killers were watched on about twenty-five occasions – sometimes not even for the whole day.

Sadly, one of the days when surveillance was not in place was Mother's Day – 9 May 1999. This was the day David Johnson was lured to Snowtown and killed.

David Johnson was a twin, but from the age of fifteen his life took a tragically different path from that of his identical sibling, Michael. The pair was born in 1975 to parents

Carlyne and Marcus Johnson. They had an older brother named Nigel.

When the twins were three, Carlyne and Marcus divorced. By 1989 Carlyne had remarried and moved across the border to Victoria, taking her sons with her. Marcus had no contact with the boys.

In his second year of high school, David Johnson began to drift off the rails. It was late 1990 when he declared his intention to return to Adelaide and live with his father.

Marcus Johnson was stunned when his son and ex-wife turned up without warning, stopping him on the footpath near his work. It was the only way they'd known how to find him.

Marcus had recently married his longtime partner Elizabeth Harvey and was at first reluctant to have his son live with him. He needed to seek his wife's permission: she already had her four sons at home. Elizabeth agreed to take David in, but only if his mother handed over furniture and cash.

Living with his father, Elizabeth Harvey and her sons was not a happy time for David Johnson. He fought with his new stepbrothers and disliked his stepmother, who would claim social security benefits for him but keep the cash for herself.

David became even more uneasy when John Bunting arrived on the scene. During regular telephone calls, David would describe to his mother how the relationship between Marcus and Elizabeth had become 'strange'. Carlyne later told police:

> Apparently on some nights, [Elizabeth's] boyfriend [John Bunting] would come around and stay the night. Marcus would go around to another house they were renting and stay the night there.

David spoke of Bunting and how he didn't like being in the house while Bunting was there. Bunting was always threatening to belt David. David fought with [Elizabeth's] kids and if he ever hit one of them she would complain to Bunting and Bunting would belt him.

David's new lifestyle was turbulent and his schoolwork suffered. During his late teens, he drifted between jobs – and homes. He lived with a girlfriend, and then moved back with his father, who had separated from Elizabeth Harvey.

In 1994 David spent time back in Victoria, first staying with his mother, then with his twin brother Michael. But by the end of that year he was again in Adelaide, living with his dad. David's stepbrothers Troy Youde and James Vlassakis were regular visitors, often staying for days at a time.

For almost all the time he lived in Adelaide, David Johnson's mother feared for her son's safety. She was plagued by nightmares in which her boy was murdered – she visualised him being strangled:

In December 1998 David came to Hamilton [Victoria] and told me how Troy [Youde] had disappeared. I asked David if he had been murdered and he said he didn't think so. He thought that Troy had run away. David and I spent a lot of time discussing Troy's disappearance.

David told me that Jamie [James Vlassakis] had said to him that Bunting had murdered someone about ten years ago and had got away with it. I tried to get David to go to the police and tell them that he thought Troy had been murdered and Bunting had murdered someone ten years earlier, but David wouldn't go. He said Jamie was on drugs and . . . no one would believe him.

During her son's Christmas visit in 1998, Carlyne's nightmares returned. Again she feared David would be murdered. Two months later, she and husband Ron travelled to Adelaide in a bid to persuade David to come home with them:

On February 28, 1999, Ron and I went to Adelaide to try and get David to come back with us ... I spoke to David about my nightmares about him getting murdered. He would say that I had been watching too much TV. I asked him whether he had heard anything from Troy and ... why not? He was starting to see my point ...

He told me Jamie had told him he had helped bury the body of a person that Bunting had killed. He didn't say where, what sex, or any other details. David did not know whether to believe Jamie or not because he was always on drugs.

David said that he made sure that he was always in a public place if Bunting was around. I said with all these things happening he should come back to Hamilton. He said that he was making arrangements to move in with Linda [his girlfriend].

Two days later, David went on an outing with his mum and stepfather.

David seemed reasonably happy that day. He had decided he would move away from his father and move in with Linda. We had our house on the market and when we sold it we would probably move back to Adelaide and he could live with us. He was looking for a job so that he would become financially independent. At 6.30 p.m. that day was the last time I saw him. I didn't hear from him again.

By May 1999 John Bunting and Mark Haydon believed the intense police pressure had subsided; that they had weathered the storm created by Elizabeth Haydon's disappearance.

In reality, undercover police operations were in full swing. Surveillance teams had been following the suspects – although not every day. Bunting and Wagner's mobile telephone records had been scrutinised to see who they'd been calling. Warrants were then obtained, allowing the suspects' homes and then mobile telephones to be tapped. By law investigators could not listen to the calls as they happened, but recordings were checked by designated 'monitors', who then passed on relevant recordings to detectives on the case. This usually occurred within twenty-four hours.

John Bunting – along with Elizabeth Harvey and her sons – had left Murray Bridge and shifted back to Adelaide, renting a house in the northern suburbs. Unaware he was being so closely monitored, Bunting's urge to kill had again surfaced. And he had chosen another victim: David Johnson.

David was living in a flat with his father, Marcus Johnson, and James Vlassakis was a regular visitor. Bunting gave Vlassakis the task of luring David Johnson to his death.

> He [Bunting] turned around and said, 'Can you go and get David for me?' And I knew what he wanted straightaway, knew what he was talking about [by] the way he asked.

Vlassakis told David Johnson about a computer being sold by a 'mate'. It was a deal too good to miss, only $200. The drawback, Vlassakis explained, was that they'd have to drive to the country to see it.

It was the evening of 9 May 1999 when James Vlassakis met with David Johnson to make the journey to

Snowtown. On the way Vlassakis dropped his mother's car at home, David following in his own vehicle.

John Bunting and Robert Wagner were already at Snowtown, waiting for their prey to arrive. At 6.40 p.m., Wagner used his mobile phone to call Vlassakis; their conversation was intercepted by police:

Wagner: *Hello, where are you?*

Vlassakis: *I'm just about at my mum's house and then we are leaving. Just taking the car home.*

Wagner: *Are you there?*

Vlassakis: *Yeah, just taking the car home, then we are leaving.*

Wagner: *Right, so you've got puss head with you?*

Vlassakis: *Yeah, he's just behind me. I'm going to get him to park around the corner from Mum's.*

Wagner: *Yeah.*

Vlassakis: *Yeah. Where's your car? Out of sight?*

Wagner: *I parked it down near Kathy's* [the Snowtown house rented by Kathy and Simon Jones].

Vlassakis: *All right. So he won't see it?*

Wagner: *Yeah.*

Vlassakis: *Yeah, okay, no dramas.*

Wagner: *Puss head's on his way, isn't he?*

Vlassakis: *Ay.*

Wagner: *Hello, hello . . .*

Vlassakis: *Yeah, it'll be just me and him.*

Wagner: *Ring me when you're leaving.*

Vlassakis: *I can't. I tried to ring you before, and it says your phone is not a contactable service.*

Wagner: *Yeah, I was inside the bank.*

Vlassakis: *Oh, right, okay. Well um, well give us a ring in ten, fifteen minutes.*

Wagner: *No, ring me.*

Vlassakis: *Ring you, all right, okay, it's easier. All right, I'm entering Mum's street now so it won't be that long, okay?*

Wagner: *All right.*

Vlassakis: *All right, I'll see you after.*

Once Vlassakis had dropped off his mother's car he joined David Johnson, telling him to drive north out of town.

At 6.56 p.m., another call was intercepted. This time it was John Bunting talking to Vlassakis:

Vlassakis: *Hello.*

Bunting: *Hello.*

Vlassakis: *Hello.*

Bunting: *This is the voice of happiness.*

Vlassakis: *Ha, ha. Yeah, um, we are on the way up there.*

Bunting: *Cool.*

Vlassakis: *Okay, so it's still all right for 200?*

Bunting: *Yeah, we'll meet you over there. We will leave the side door open for you.*

Vlassakis: *Okay.*

Bunting: *Just walk straight in, okay?*

Vlassakis: *Yeah, the machine all set up is it?*

Bunting: *Yeah.*

Vlassakis: *Yeah, cool, no drama. Okay, we'll see you when we get up there.*

Bunting: *No worries, bye.*

Vlassakis: *Take it easy.*

Vlassakis and David Johnson arrived a little over an hour later, parking outside the old bank. They strolled through a gate along the side of the building, Vlassakis accidentally kicking a piece of metal and causing a loud crash. The elderly lady who lived in the former bank manager's residence peered out her window. Vlassakis gave her a wave as he and Johnson entered the bank's side door.

Inside a computer was sitting on the floor, set up and switched on. John Bunting was standing nearby, clearly visible, but Robert Wagner was out of sight. James Vlassakis walked towards the computer:

> John said hello and then I went to the computer, said to David, 'This is the computer, come and have a look.'
>
> As I turned around, Robert had David around the throat and John was putting the handcuffs onto David.

David Johnson was led into a small partitioned area which had once been the bank manager's office. An old TV being stored in the building was lifted into the room, and David was forced to sit on it.

Frightened, David asked Bunting, 'What's going on?'

'You're right,' was the reply. Once David had answered some questions, Bunting told him, 'You're going home in half an hour.'

Vlassakis played along, knowing only too well that David Johnson would not be going home:

> He [David] was asking a lot of questions and he was ... panicking and his legs were shaking and that – just shaking. I mean, you could see him shaking and he was shaking all over, and he was looking around; didn't know what was going on.
>
> David ... asked me if he was going to go home. I said, 'Yes.' He said, 'Do you promise?' and I said, 'Yes, I promise', and that was it.

Handcuffed, confused and perched on the old TV, David

Johnson was forced to hand over his wallet. Bunting rifled through its contents, pausing to examine the bank keycard, demanding to know David's PIN. Next Bunting's computer was shifted into the small room, its microphone perched on a cardboard box in front of the prisoner.

During past murders Bunting had forced his victims to repeat phrases – some abusive – which were later tape-recorded and played on the telephone to family and friends, creating the impression that the victims had not vanished but had run away. This time Bunting had devised a more high-tech approach. He would use his computer, with a special software program, to record David Johnson's voice, forcing the victim to recite numbers, names, words and even full sentences. Bunting could then piece them together electronically.

John Bunting presided over the recording session as Wagner held a notebook for David to read from. It was Vlassakis's job to activate the recordings. The first commenced at 8.41 p.m.:

1, 2, 3, 4, 5, 6, 7, 8, 9, 10, 20, 30, 40, 50, 60, 70, 80, 90 100
 Greg, Tom, Paul, Roger, Steven, Paul, John, Robert, Fred, Chris, Adrian, Marcus, Amanda, Tony, Darren, Robbie, Nicole, Tina, Jenny, Michael, David, Nigel, Helen, Tracey, George, Brad, Bradley, Joe, Ben, Barry, Vanessa, Eddie, George, Colin, Mitchell, Michael, Adam, Len, Clint, Alan, Peter, Josh, Randy, Ray, Raymond, Kathy, Kathy, Karen, Julie, Fiona, Lisa, Tammy, Vicky, Troy, Dillon, James, Evonne, Simone, Toby, Kathy, Kathleen, Emma, Trisha, Trish, Teresa, Heather, Emmanuel, Linda, Trevor.

These were the names of as many of David's family and friends as Bunting could think of. Next came words and phrases which could be used to link or create sentences in David Johnson's voice:

> And, not, no, never, soon, too soon, can, can't, yes, yeah, yer, maybe, no, nup, fuck off, could be, could, do, don't, I, want, need, needing, am, ing, in, computer, hay, hey, heey, service, them, come, go, stick, stuff, fuck, fuck you, fuck off shit head, on, off, why, if, what, when, where, who, say, shit, so what, so, was, watch me, hotel, pub, hey, fuck off shit head, no.

John Bunting then reeled off dozens of sentences which David Johnson was ordered to repeat. Among them:

> Fuck off.
> Piss off shithead.
> How many times do you need to be fucking told?
> Why are you phoning me?
> Never phone me again.
> If I never see you again it will be too soon.
> You're not my brother, you're a waste.
> Your mother's a whore.
> This is David, I'm not here right now, leave your name and shit and I'll get back to you.

Some of the recordings were intended for specific people. If Bunting wasn't happy with David's delivery, he would order him to 'do it again'.

> Marcus, I'm going to Perth.
> Toni, I've fucked my car up, when you see Jamie tell him to meet me at Roger's.
> Tell Amanda to eat shit and die.

The recordings continued for almost an hour before Bunting and Wagner began their murderous ritual. Music was played in the background – again the Live album *Throwing Copper*.

Back inside the small manager's office, black plastic sheets were spread over the floor. Forced to lie on the plastic, David Johnson's jeans were removed and his T-shirt was cut from his body with a knife. His shoes and socks were also removed, one of the socks stuffed into his mouth and silver duct tape wrapped around his head to hold the gag in place. Vlassakis stood back as Wagner and Bunting let fly with a savage attack:

> That's when Robert walked up to David and put David's head in between his knees and started hitting David on the back . . . just kept hitting and hitting and hitting.
>
> Then it just became like a frenzy. After Robert started hitting into David, John jumped on – went down on the floor and started grabbing . . . David's legs. Then he said to help him, because David was starting to kick and that; told me to get down and help him. I got down there and grabbed the other leg of David. John hit David in the balls. John told me to hit him so I hit him.

As quickly and suddenly as it had started, the beating stopped. Wagner sifted through a plastic bag sitting nearby, retrieving rubber gloves, cigarette lighters and boxes of sparklers. Before the torture began, however, Bunting had a task for his accomplices; he wanted to be sure David Johnson hadn't lied about his banking details, so the bankcard and PIN would have to be tested. Bunting wrote the PIN on Vlassakis's hand, before ordering him and Wagner to drive to a service station at nearby Port Wakefield to test the card.

Robert sat on about 160 [kilometres per hour] or so. He really thrashed it going down there. Really, really fast and I thought he was going to lose the car because ... it was going all over the road.

We arrived at the service station, I said to Robert, 'Go in there and use the card', but he didn't want to, so we – I went in but Robert went in behind me.

And I asked the guy there at the front [counter], I just said, 'Can I try this for five dollars?' and he just swiped the card and I put in the PIN number, and it just came back, 'Not authorised, cancelled'.

As Vlassakis and Wagner returned to the car, Vlassakis spoke to Bunting via mobile telephone. Like the calls made earlier that night, it was intercepted by police:

Bunting: *Hello.*
Vlassakis: *Hello.*
Bunting: *How is it?*
Vlassakis: *Um, says not authorised, cancelled.*
Bunting: *Oh, in other words [not audible] broke, there's no money.*
Vlassakis: *Yeah, I tried to phone.*
Bunting: *Okay.*
Vlassakis: *It's okay.*
Bunting: *Hello.*
Vlassakis: *Hello.*
(Call interrupted by poor reception)
Bunting: *Where are you?*
Vlassakis: *Um, Port Wakefield.*
Bunting: *Get back here.*
Vlassakis: *Okay, see you in five.*
Bunting: *No worries.*
Vlassakis: *See ya.*

When Vlassakis and Wagner returned to the bank they entered through the side door. David Johnson was lying on the black plastic, face down. He was dead, a belt looped around his neck.

While alone with John Bunting, David had courageously decided to fight for his life. He had manoeuvred his shackled hands to the front of his body and a violent scuffle had erupted, the killer suffering cracked ribs as he was kicked by his would-be victim.

David lunged for a Stanley knife lying on the floor, forcing Bunting to retreat. Knowing full well Wagner was out, Bunting called out to his friend to 'come here'. The distraction worked, and as David glanced towards the door, worried that Wagner had returned, Bunting overpowered him.

Using the victim's own belt, John Bunting choked the last breath out of David Johnson – the force of the stranglehold so great, Bunting crushed his thumb.

The pain from his injured ribs was acute, and John Bunting struggled as he unlocked the vault door, manipulating the lock with a piece of bent wire. Bunting told Vlassakis he would have to help Robert Wagner with the body.

> Robert then said to me that it would have to be a 'slice and dice' and there would be a lot of blood involved. And John was saying, 'You're going to have to do it' – they were both talking to me.

As Wagner and Vlassakis carried David Johnson's body, Bunting removed a strip of tape to open the slit in the black plastic which covered the vault's entrance. Bunting instructed Vlassakis to put on the white overalls he normally wore while working inside the vault. Bunting referred to the overalls as his 'playsuit'.

> He went and got that, and told me to put that on. So I had to take my clothes off down to my jocks and put that over the top.
>
> Robert got me to put gloves on and that before we carried David into the vault, so I was wearing gloves. Robert Wagner had gloves.
>
> When we were in the vault, Robert lifted the barrel [lids] and chose one. David was laying [sic] on the floor … Robert grabbed his keys and took the handcuffs off David.
>
> We lifted David into the barrel headfirst and Robert grabbed knives which were on the … lounge that was in there.
>
> Robert grabbed the knife and told me to hold David's leg and he started cutting David at the knee. I wasn't watching Robert all the time cutting it … too gross … couldn't watch it. As he was cutting … I could see quite clearly that David was just going to fit in there without having to cut and I told Robert that he was going to fit.

John Bunting stuck his head through the slit in the plastic sheets covering the vault entrance. He warned the pair that they had an unexpected visitor.

Simon Jones had visited the bank that night out of curiosity. As he would later detail in a police interview, Jones had dropped his wife at a nearby town, returning home about 10.30 p.m.:

> I noticed there was a note on my front door at home; it asked me to ring Robert's mobile phone number. There

was a number on the piece of paper, I rang that number and spoke to John Bunting. I asked John where he was and he told me he was in Snowtown. He told me he was only a couple of minutes away and that he would be over soon. I got curious about what he said, so I went over to the bank, I used my key to get in the side door, I opened it but the chain was attached on the inside.

I called out, and John came to the side door and let me in. I went through into the main area of the bank and I saw that he had his computer on the floor. John then said, 'Come and have a look at this'; he wanted me to have a look at some programs that he had on the computer.

As he looked at Bunting's computer, Simon Jones's attention was drawn to the bizarre screensaver displayed on the monitor:

It started off as a picture of a graveyard, and then all these skeletons dig themselves out of the graves and then start running around the graveyard bumping into things.

About one or two minutes after I sat down at the computer, Jamie Vlassakis walked out of the vault. The door was open. I could see the black plastic and that there was a slit ... you could see the [vault] wall through the slit in the plastic.

As Jamie walked out I could see he was wearing overalls, white overalls, I think they were disposable. I don't recall the exact conversation with him, but at some stage, I think as I was about to leave, Jamie said, 'Give me a hug'. He took a step towards me and put his arms up as though he was going to hug me. I just said, 'Get lost.' He stank of the rotting meat. When he said this to me, he was laughing. I noticed that he had some gloves on.

I saw Robert Wagner walk out of the vault; he was wearing his yellow CFS overalls – Country Fire Service overalls. He had gloves on too. He had a very strange look on his face; he was staring at me intensely. Thinking back ... I think he may have thought that I had seen something that I shouldn't have.

After Robert gave me that stare, I talked to John for a bit and then, as I was leaving, Robert said, 'Give us a hug.' I told him to 'piss off'. He chuckled, John then opened the door and I said I would see them later and I went back home.

With Simon Jones out of the way, Robert Wagner emerged once again from the vault, telling Bunting he had a 'surprise'. He held up a surgical glove with a piece of human flesh inside. It had been sliced from one of David Johnson's legs.

James Vlassakis felt ill as he walked with Bunting and Wagner across to Simon Jones's house. Wagner was carrying the flesh in the glove. Inside the house, Vlassakis was first to take a shower.

When I walked out of the shower, I put on the clothes that I was wearing before and I put the 'playsuit' – of John's – into a plastic bag. When I got to the kitchen, Robert was cooking the part of David in the fry pan. He cut it up into square pieces and put it in the fry pan and it was cooking. John said to me that I had to try it, he was laughing... and I didn't want to, but I had to because John said that. I grabbed a small piece – the smallest piece on the plate and ate it.

They gave some to Simon from that fry pan and John had some, Robert had some. Robert had a couple of pieces and there was still some left on the plate.

Simon Jones was completely unaware what he was eating. He would later tell police he believed it had been road-kill kangaroo.

> Robert fried up some meat in the fry pan. He told me that it was some kangaroo that they had hit on the way up to Snowtown. It was red meat – about a three inch by six inch piece of steak – it looked like kangaroo steak to me.
>
> He carried it into the house contained in a surgical glove. The open end of the glove had been tied up; he had to open the glove to put the meat in the pan. I know that he put garlic into the pan…he had been hunting around the kitchen looking for the garlic.
>
> He was cooking it for about ten minutes (and) was going to feed it to the dogs, he said that he had cooked it too quickly and it had gone a bit rubbery. I stopped him and cut off a piece to try it, so I could make a suggestion on how he could make it better next time. My parents had cooked kangaroo before and they seemed to know how to do it.
>
> It was a bit chewy…I told him that he stuffed it up pretty well.

In the days after David Johnson's murder, John Bunting concocted a story to explain his victim's disappearance. He instructed James Vlassakis to begin spreading the lie among David's family and friends.

They were told that David had taken up with a thirteen-year-old girl who'd fallen pregnant and, to make matters worse, he'd crashed his car and was hiding from the police. Among the first to be told the tale was David's father, Marcus Johnson.

Two days after the murder, Bunting sent Vlassakis to the

flat Marcus Johnson had shared with his son. James told Marcus the cover story, claiming David had asked him to fetch clothes and documents he needed to claim his unemployment pension.

Vlassakis delivered the papers to John Bunting and, days later, returned to the flat with Robert Wagner to gather up David's furniture.

Others to be told the false story by James Vlassakis were the two girls David Johnson had been seeing at the same time – unbeknownst to each other. The more recent of the girlfriends, Amanda, was puzzled by David's sudden disappearance; so too her close friend Toni, who had introduced the couple. The girls were more upset when Toni received two bizarre phone calls, apparently from David himself:

My phone rang and when I picked it I heard a male voice speak and he said, 'Toni you're a fucking liar.'

I said, 'What, who is this?' He then said, 'Toni you're a fucking liar, is Amanda there?'

I said, 'No, who is this?' There was silence for a couple of seconds and then the phone hung up. I did not recognise the voice on the phone.

After I hung up I rang Amanda and spoke to her for a couple of minutes and then, as soon as I hung up from her, the phone rang again. I answered it and heard the same male voice.

This time I recognised the voice as David's but it sounded to me like it was being played on an answering machine.

David's long-term girlfriend, Linda, had last seen him on Mother's Day – the day of his murder:

David had stayed at my home overnight Saturday 8 May and left at about 12.30 p.m. on the Sunday. When he left he told me that he was going to pick up a computer somewhere north of Gawler. He said he was buying it from a contact provided by his stepbrother Jamie [Vlassakis]. I don't know exactly where he was going but he made the comment, 'Knowing Jamie it's probably two hours past Gawler', something along those lines.

He told me his stepmother's de facto, John Bunting, had a computer and that he wanted one like that. He said that he was to pay $200 to the person selling the computer and $200 to Jamie for providing the contact.

I remember thinking at the time that it was a cheap price and I thought the computer may be stolen. I told David to be careful about what he may be getting himself into and he replied, 'I'm all right.'

Four days later, when she hadn't heard from David, Linda and her mother visited his flat. Vlassakis and Wagner were there, collecting some of David's property. Linda spoke to Vlassakis at the door:

On arrival I knocked at the front door. Jamie answered and we spoke.

'Is David there?'

'No, I haven't seen him.'

'He told me he was going with you Sunday night.'

'He's at a friend's place, why?'

'Because I'm his girlfriend and I'm worried about him.'

'Why? He says he hasn't seen you for three or four years.'

'You're joking?'

'No, he's got a thirteen-year-old girl pregnant and he's seeing someone else.'

Upset and uneasy, Linda didn't know what to believe:

> Before I left the flat that day I told Jamie to tell David to call me. I said I would call the police and report David missing if I didn't get a call.

The threat prompted a hasty telephone call from Vlassakis to Bunting, which was recorded by police:

Vlassakis: *Guess who I had a visit from.*

Bunting: *Who?*

Vlassakis: *Linda and her mum.*

Bunting: *Who, Linda?*

Vlassakis: *Yeah.*

Bunting: *Yeah, what about it?*

Vlassakis: *Don't you know David's been going out with her for eight years?*

Bunting: *For eight years.*

Vlassakis: *Yep, and still going out with her.*

Bunting: *Did you tell her the good news?*

Vlassakis: *Yeah, I said that David was going out with this bird Amanda in the flats. He is going out with Jenny as well, who's thirteen and pregnant.*

Bunting: *Yeah.*

Vlassakis: *If David doesn't ring her tonight or today sometime . . .*

Bunting: *Yeah . . .*

Vlassakis: *They are going to call the police tomorrow.*

Bunting: *Cool, that's okay.*

Vlassakis: *Okay?*

Bunting: *Okay.*

Vlassakis: *They want to hear his voice to make sure he's all right.*

Bunting: *Oh, no dramas.*

His computer equipped with an array of recordings in David Johnson's voice, Bunting set about designing a passage which could be played to the troublesome Linda.

He called Vlassakis to give the recording a test run. This exchange too was tapped by police:

Bunting: *While I've got you on the phone, just listen to this, okay . . . let me find it.*

David Johnson recording is played: *Fuck off. Hey this is David. Linda how fucken hard is it? I'm not interested, fuck off.*

Bunting: *How did that sound?*

Vlassakis: *Yeah, it just has to be a bit louder, a bit closer, sounds a bit hollow.*

The conversation continued while Bunting experimented with the recording, trying to make it sound more genuine. David Johnson's voice, however, was never played to Linda. Bunting devised an alternative plan.

On Bunting's instruction, Vlassakis bought a prepaid mobile phone and then gave Linda the number, telling her she could use it to contact David.

Bunting had arranged for his girlfriend, Gail Sinclair, to answer the call, posing as David's 'new' young lover. Sinclair had no idea she was concealing a murder.

When Linda called the mobile phone number, she encountered a nervous female voice on the other end of the line:

I said, 'Hello, is David there?'
    She said, 'Who is this?'
    I said, 'A friend, Lyn.'
    She called out, 'David, David', as if calling out to him.

She spoke to me again and said, 'He must be on the toilet, I've got to go now, bye.'

She then hung up.

Linda again dialled the mobile later that day, leaving a voicemail message asking David to call. Her next attempt was seven days later – amid news reports that bodies had been found in barrels in an old Snowtown bank.

PART THREE

JUSTICE

TWENTY-TWO

'Never before in the history of South Australia has the challenge been so great – to investigate a series of crimes as a single event.'

South Australia's Acting Police Commissioner, Neil McKenzie, delivered these words to a packed media conference. Sitting alongside him was the Major Crime boss, Detective Superintendent Paul Schramm. It was 24 May 1999, and the pair had just announced the formation of Taskforce Chart. A team of thirty-three officers, headed by Paul Schramm, was to investigate the worst case of serial killing in Australian history.

'We have taken this extraordinary step in bringing all our skills together in one place at the one time [the taskforce]. It doesn't have a finish date, but it certainly has a problem to contend with.'

Within weeks, the task force had uncovered what it suspected were twelve murders. The remains of eight victims had been found in barrels, hidden in the vault of an old bank building in the small community of Snowtown. Two more bodies were then found buried in the back yard of a suburban house. In addition, investigators had linked to the case a skeleton found in a paddock almost five years before and the death of a young man which had previously – and mistakenly – been deemed a suicide. Responsible was a group of killers which had even 'preyed on themselves'.

The 'Snowtown Murders', as they were dubbed within hours of the story breaking, attracted almost instant national and international media coverage. Journalists from every major Australian newspaper, television and radio station were churning out stories on the latest developments, sniffing around for a new angle, an 'exclusive'.

The story was carried by media outlets around the world, receiving most attention in nearby Asia, the United Kingdom and United States. In London, BBC news coverage included live updates from Australia. Four days after the story broke, the *Hong Kong Standard* ran with the headline 'Acid-vat killings worst on record'. In the United States, where serial killers are more common than they are in the land 'Down Under', one news service compared the murders with serial killings in California in the mid-1980s. In both cases, the newspaper claimed, the motive had been social security fraud – killing for pensions.

A television crew rushed to Adelaide from Japan, only to find that their initial information had been incorrect: one of the victims was, in fact, not a Japanese backpacker. They promptly flew home.

Paul Schramm, a veteran cop and lecturer in the management of serious crime, had expected the media avalanche. What's more, he had planned for it, even consulting the commander of Britain's 'House of Horrors' case on how to handle the information flow.

With three men charged and before the courts, it was a sensitive process. Within days of the Snowtown discovery, police and the Director of Public Prosecutions, Paul Rofe QC, were becoming concerned about the media's activities.

They were worried that the eventual trials of the accused would be prejudiced by the widespread media coverage. Some reporters were nosing around in areas the police had yet to cover. Rofe took the unprecedented step of calling a media conference to warn journalists about their legal obligations in covering the story. A media release was issued immediately afterwards:

> The Director of Public Prosecutions, Paul Rofe QC, today issued a warning to all media outlets that prosecutions for contempt of court would follow if the media published material which tended to prejudice the prosecution or defence ...
>
> Persons charged with criminal offences are presumed innocent until and unless their guilt is established beyond reasonable doubt after a fair trial according to law. Trial by media will not be tolerated under any circumstances.

Apart from the sheer magnitude of the so-called Snowtown Murders and the public's fascination with serial killing in general, the Australian media had another reason to be attracted to this story: South Australia's reputation for bizarre murders.

One newspaper had gone so far as to brand South Australia the 'Little State of Horrors'.

In the early 1980s, long before the bank vault discovery, world-renowned author Salman Rushdie visited the state's capital, Adelaide, known as the 'City of Churches'. Rushdie later wrote that Adelaide is a perfect setting for a horror novel or film, because sleepy, conservative towns are the sorts of places where such things happen.

Adelaide's reputation had begun with the 1972 murder of homosexual university lecturer Dr George Duncan. He was set upon by a group of men prowling the banks of the River Torrens, near the heart of the city, which was a known haunt for homosexuals. Duncan, along with another man, was thrown into the river. With only one lung, as a result of tuberculosis, Duncan drowned. Three police officers, members of the Vice Squad who'd been at a colleague's farewell drinking session, were charged with manslaughter fourteen years later. The charges were laid only after a coronial inquest, two local police investigations and a probe by detectives from Scotland Yard. All three accused were eventually acquitted.

In June 1979, nine years after the Duncan drowning, teenager Alan Barnes disappeared. A week later his body was found on the banks of a river northeast of Adelaide. Barnes, seventeen, had died of blood loss caused by a shocking injury to his anus. Barnes was to be the first of five young men to become victims of the so-called 'Family' murders between 1979 and 1983. All were abducted, drugged, sexually abused and mutilated. The final victim, fifteen-year-old Richard Kelvin, was kept alive by his captor or captors for as long as five weeks before being murdered.

To this day suspicions remain that the killings were the work of a gang of men dubbed 'The Family'. Only one man was ever convicted, and for only one of the killings, that of Richard Kelvin. In 1984 Bevan Spencer von Einem was sentenced to life in prison. Four years later, von Einem was also charged with the murders of Barnes and eighteen-year-old Mark Langley, another of the Family victims. Those charges were dropped after vital evidence was ruled inadmissible.

Three years before the first Family murder, another spate of serial killings had begun in South Australia. The abduction, sexual assault and murder of seven young women in late 1976 and early 1977 were to become known as the Truro murders. Two men were responsible for these killings: a bisexual named Christopher Worrell and his lover, James Miller. Worrell was killed in a car crash in February 1977, but Miller was later charged with the seven murders and convicted of six. He subsequently wrote a book claiming he had been infatuated with, yet frightened by, the much younger Worrell, who was actually responsible for the killings. Miller claimed his crime was not murder; he was merely driving the car while Worrell picked up the victims.

So then, in 1999, when the bodies were discovered at Snowtown, South Australia was once more being judged from outside – and from within – as some kind of meeting place for perverse murderers. On the day he announced the formation of Taskforce Chart, a reporter asked Acting Commissioner McKenzie about South Australia's 'reputation'.

'My impression of this is that it is not out of keeping with unusual and bizarre things that happen around the world,' he replied. 'What the media tends to do in these circumstances is to get out the record books and produce a chronicle of unusual or bizarre crimes that have occurred in one place or another.'

One thing was for certain, though: no amount of searching through Australia's criminal history would find a crime quite as staggering, or as gruesome, as this.

In South Australia the wheels of justice move slowly, and the sheer magnitude of the Snowtown serial killings case served only to retard the wheels even further. At times they even threatened to come to a grinding halt. While Bunting, Haydon and Wagner were arrested in May 1999, and Vlassakis the following month, the committal hearing for the four accused did not begin for another nineteen months.

Typically a committal hearing is designed to test the evidence against an accused. Such hearings are presided over by magistrates, who must decide whether or not the evidence before them is strong enough for the accused to stand trial in a higher court.

It was 11 December 2000 when the Snowtown committal hearing began. By this time detectives from the police Chart taskforce had amassed a mountain of evidence; enough, they believed, to charge Bunting, Wagner and Haydon with ten of the twelve murders and Vlassakis with five.

During the Snowtown committal, sixty-eight witnesses were called and a staggering 1458 witness statements – known as declarations – were tendered. The hearing lasted a marathon eight months.

For prosecutors the committal was a tumultuous affair during which they were dealt two significant blows. The first was the exposure of major shortfalls in the evidence linking Mark Haydon to many of the murders. It was becoming clear that his role in the crimes had been a peripheral one – he was no prime mover. It seemed almost certain that Haydon's legal team would use later pre-trial hearings in the Supreme Court to attack the prosecution case. It became apparent, too, that Haydon's lawyers would almost certainly launch a bid to have several murder charges dismissed while seeking a separate trial on any remaining charges.

Second, a star witness for the prosecution died during the committal before being able to give evidence. Elizabeth Harvey was the mother of accused James Vlassakis and victim Troy Youde and the stepmother of victim David

Johnson. She had been Bunting's partner of five years. Harvey's evidence would have been critical: she had helped Bunting steal money from victims' bank accounts but had been granted immunity in return for her testimony.

Elizabeth Harvey died of cancer on 5 February 2001. She had been diagnosed with the disease less than two years before – in the same month as the bodies in the barrels were discovered by police.

However, despite this setback, and almost on cue, prosecutors were able to add to their arsenal an even stronger witness: one of the killers themselves.

It was Thursday, 19 June 2001, and the Snowtown committal was under way, although this morning it had been adjourned. Instead the media was gathering outside South Australia's Supreme Court, just across the road. The legal precinct was abuzz with rumours of a major development in the Snowtown case. Inside, the courtroom was packed with media, detectives and victims' families.

James Vlassakis's lawyer, Rosemary Davey QC, stood alongside the dock as her client responded to each charge as it was read aloud.

'You are charged that between August 25 and September 8, 1998, at Snowtown or another place, you murdered Troy Youde.'

Vlassakis's response was swift: 'Guilty.'

'You are charged that between September 16 and September 24, 1998, at Snowtown or another place, you murdered Fred Brooks.'

'Guilty.'

'You are charged that between October 27 and November 24, 1998, at Snowtown or another place, you murdered Gary O'Dwyer.'

'Guilty.'

'You are charged that between May 8 and May 13, 1999, at Snowtown you murdered David Johnson.'

'Guilty.'

As he pleaded his guilt in the horrendous crimes, Vlassakis wiped tears from his eyes and his voice began to waver. The final plea was delivered in a whisper. He slumped back into his seat as a court official again read aloud:

'James Vlassakis, you have pleaded guilty to four counts of murder.'

Vlassakis stood as Justice Brian Martin delivered sentence:

'The law prescribes only one penalty for the crime of murder, and that is life imprisonment. Accordingly, for each of the four counts on which you have pleaded guilty, I sentence you to imprisonment for life. I will now hear further submissions about a non-parole period.'

Vlassakis's admissions stunned those on the periphery of the case, as well as the defence teams for his co-accused. Behind the scenes, however, the guilty pleas had been a long time coming. A deal had been done between prosecutors and Vlassakis's lawyers. While Vlassakis maintained his innocence in the murder of Gavin Porter – the charge was later withdrawn – he pleaded guilty to four other killings. He would also become the Crown's star witness, testifying against his co-accused.

James Vlassakis was hoping the truth would set him free. In return for his cooperation the young man was given the prospect that, one day, he would be released from prison on parole.

★　★　★

The end of the Snowtown committal hearing came just under a month later, with Magistrate David Gurry setting the stage for one – or even two – of the most sensational criminal trials in Australia's legal history.

'Over a number of months, having had the opportunity to consider the declarations and consider the oral evidence of various witnesses, I have formed the view that the evidence is sufficient to place each of the defendants on trial for each of the offences as charged and I accordingly rule to that end.'

TWENTY-THREE

South Australian law dictates that the crime of murder is punishable with a mandatory sentence of life imprisonment. However, in each case the judge has the power to set a non-parole period, after which time the offender can be considered for conditional release from jail. Defence lawyers, along with the prosecution, make submissions as to the appropriate length of the non-parole period.

Under the terms of Vlassakis's deal – kept secret until the last possible moment – the prosecution had agreed not to oppose the setting of a non-parole period, in return for Vlassakis's guilty pleas and testimony against Bunting, Wagner and Haydon.

Amid fears for his safety after he'd decided to turn star witness, James Vlassakis was shifted to another jail and given a new identity. The media was forbidden from showing his image within South Australia: there was a risk that other inmates would not take kindly to someone who'd turned informer – among prison inmates he would have been branded a 'dog' and targeted with violence.

Sentencing submissions for James Vlassakis, before Justice Kevin Duggan, began eight months after the guilty pleas. It was the job of defence counsel Rosemary Davey to present a spirited case as to why her client should one day be released into the community.

'On the twenty-first of June last year [2001], James Vlassakis pleaded guilty to four counts of murder. I said at that time he has, by his pleas, acknowledged his involvement in horrific crimes; but they were more than that. The events leading to the death of four people were evil, marked by unparalleled barbarism, cruelty and sadism. That these acts have affected so many people and the whole community of South Australia, there can be no doubt at all.

'But the story of James Spyridon Vlassakis is not the story of an evil young man. It is the story of a person who participated in evil and why he did so. I can hear the sceptics say, "Oh, another tale of a hard-done-by life to excuse criminal behaviour". But this man had an appalling and completely dysfunctional upbringing, a complete absence of what some people would call a normal life. Sexual abuse, a lack of appropriate intervention and care for him. The submissions on behalf of my client tell the story of a relationship between a teenage boy and the man who filled the role of a father. That man was John Bunting.

'John Bunting is a depraved, disturbed if not a deranged, vicious and dangerous killer. The relationship was one of power and corruption of my client. This young man had the courage to speak to police initially and, over time, broke the bonds of John Bunting and pleaded guilty.'

As she stood before the court, Rosemary Davey detailed James Vlassakis's tragic life. His sexual abuse as a child, his mother's mental illness and, finally, his involvement with John Bunting.

'James Vlassakis liked, even loved, John Bunting. He thought John Bunting was intelligent, well spoken and polite; he had an air of authority and power. He worshipped John Bunting. He was a hero ... the only father figure he had. John Bunting encouraged James

Vlassakis to consider resuming his schooling. In 1995/96 he attempted to return to adult education.

'At first blush it was not an abusive relationship; it appeared to be a benign, if not positive relationship. They were going riding on his BMW motorbike together, they would go to movies together and they got on well.

'He [Vlassakis] noticed some things that he thought were strange. He noticed that John Bunting would go into people's rooms while they weren't there and search through their room. He noticed John Bunting had an obsession with guns, at one point in time John Bunting had about ten guns; he also had a silencer.

'He came to experience a number of incidents when John Bunting killed animals, dogs and cats, when James Vlassakis was present. Over a period he was desensitised to violence towards animals, violent talk towards people who were targets of animosity, such as paedophiles; acts of aggression towards those people and eventually acts of violence. It was similar to the sort of initiation performed by paedophiles on young children. It was part of John Bunting's approval of him that he engaged in those activities.

'What's psychiatrically important is this progression of violence. Constant discussion about sexual abuse. John Bunting said he was a victim of sexual abuse himself as a child by someone outside his family. It wasn't just a discussion about sexual abuse. John Bunting encouraged violent discussion about retribution against paedophiles and not just paedophiles, homosexuals. This was so much a part of their relationship; my client says it was daily conversations. Elizabeth Harvey, people who casually knew him [Bunting], all commented about his expressed hatred and comments with respect to paedophiles. His obsession was so great that in the house at 203 Waterloo Corner Road he devoted a wall to collecting references to paedophiles. What was actually created was something like a web with yellow Post–it stickers, sometimes photos, and pieces of wool connecting various people. Witnesses also talk about him discussing paedophiles and paedophilia. He also collected information about paedophiles, contact phone numbers and other information. He would keep typed dossiers on people, including on Barry Lane. This process was well under way when Vlassakis moved in. Vlassakis spent a lot of time at the house sleeping on the sofa bed or the floor. Vlassakis added some details to the chart on the wall and it grew over a period of time. Vlassakis was on social security.

'In about 1996 Elizabeth Harvey, along with Kris and Adrian, moved into 203 Waterloo Corner Road. The chart was taken down because she objected to it.

'Bunting would randomly choose a paedophile from the chart, and call them and abuse them on the phone. However he did mix with Barry Lane on a regular basis and that's how he met [Robert] Wagner. Lane was a source of information to him about paedophiles and the links between them. Bunting spoke a lot about protecting children. Bunting and Vlassakis would go and graffiti the houses of paedophiles and pour brake fluid on cars. In addition to the harassment of alleged paedophiles and damaging of property, John Bunting enlisted James Vlassakis to larceny and other offences, breaking and entering. Elizabeth Harvey would turn a blind eye. It was referred to as 'going shopping'. She would know James Vlassakis was going out with John Bunting for that purpose.

'James Vlassakis gradually became afraid of John Bunting. He maintained an emotional bond with him, but he became afraid. There was talk of violence, there was talk of paedophiles and what they deserved, and then there was talk of killing; of a man he ... now knows of as Ray Davies. John Bunting talked about killing lots of people. Vlassakis found it difficult to tell if he was serious.

'Ray Davies was killed in late 1995, early 1996. James Vlassakis learned about it some time later. James Vlassakis says from that time on, John Bunting talked about killing regularly. A small number of the people he talked about killing were actually killed, to James Vlassakis's knowledge.

'James Vlassakis was told by John Bunting and Elizabeth Harvey of the killing of Ray Davies and her involvement. He was told that Davies was buried in the back yard at 203 Waterloo Corner Road. Clinton Trezise was actually murdered at an earlier time [July to August 1992]. "Happy Pants" — my client heard reference to the killing of someone known as "Happy Pants".

'Ray Davies is the first murder my client heard of but he didn't see evidence of it and wasn't sure whether or not it was real. He heard that his mother was involved with John Bunting and Robert Wagner. That the man [Davies] had been taken from a place, taken out into the countryside, beaten, taken back to the place at Waterloo Corner Road and Ray Davies was apparently tortured and murdered and buried in the back garden.

'It wasn't until he saw the body of Gavin Porter at 3 Burdekin Avenue, Murray Bridge, with John Bunting and Robert Wagner, that he realised what was talked about was a reality. Porter was a friend of his.

'After that, and certainly by the time he became involved in the murder of Troy Youde, he was frightened and terrified he would become a victim of John Bunting, and that was part of the factors influencing him.'

Vlassakis's lawyer went on to detail the twelve murders, highlighting her client's limited role. The killings and the torture had been in progress before Vlassakis was enlisted. Not once did he instigate the torture or murder of a victim.

'Why was Vlassakis involved if he wasn't mad? And he wasn't. Our client's not evil, not motivated by evil. Why didn't he tell, why didn't he run away? In the first record of interview [with police] he was cross-examined about that very issue. He was put through the grill. He talks about this fear, a fear that his mother would be harmed. It's not necessarily something he himself can answer. The relationship can't be looked at from the perspective of an ordinary person.

'Firstly, there was this relationship with John Bunting. It was one of dependency and John Bunting himself is demonstrated as being highly manipulative. My client is young; he was eighteen, nearly nineteen, and also a serious drug user. His abuse of drugs amplified his dependency.

'Secondly there was his mother. She was involved. She had participated in the killing of Ray Davies. His mother was physically ill from early 1998 onwards. She was also mentally ill. Any disclosure would potentially disclose his mother's involvement.

'There was fear. My client had seen the torture. He had seen the killings. He knew more than one person was involved. He felt the more involved the safer he was – he was part of the group and unlikely to be a target.

'There was a lack of knowledge of what he could effectively do or where he could go. In the life and environment my client grew up in, the police were culturally the enemy.

'He didn't have another significant adult he could trust and rely on. Vlassakis was a heavy drug user and Bunting hated drug use and had referred to him as a "waste". This amplified fears he could be a target.'

Vlassakis's cooperation with the police was also detailed

in full, for the first time. Ms Davey told how her client, with the help of another lawyer, had gone to police in the days after Bunting's arrest, offering information about the murders. Vlassakis's mother did the same. Both were promised consideration of immunity.

'The statements made by Elizabeth Harvey and James Vlassakis were privileged and not to be disclosed without an order of the court.

'The [Vlassakis] interview can only be described as harrowing from anyone's point of view. He was visibly crying and distressed. He was vomiting during part of the interview. At times he was cross-examined. Police were confronted with information beyond their wildest expectations. Notwithstanding the harrowing nature of the interview, my client continued and continued. During that interview process my client's distress was so great he was unable to continue any longer. He took an overdose of heroin.

'There is a record of a telephone intercept between James Vlassakis and Elizabeth Harvey which shows his absolute distress. These were not the words of a callous killer. This is a young man whose life is out of control. It's an unvarnished expression of anguish.

'He continued using drugs throughout this time. Even at the police station. James Vlassakis found it very difficult to face another human being and admit what he had been involved in. He did not know or understand his guilt of murder because he didn't physically kill. Of course, he knew his participation was wrong. His position is that in respect of the four murders he never wished to be involved at all, including that of Troy Youde ... one thing drew him into another.

'A lot of the [evidence] arises from information provided by James Vlassakis. Particularly, he told police of how the victims were brought to their deaths, and always it was in the context of paedophiles, or a person was a "dirty" and in some way deserved to die. John Bunting used to say regularly, "I can tell a paedophile by looking at him."

'My client details how these people died and the nature and extent of the torture. He also told police of Bunting's delight in watching the victims and the process undertaken in the torturing of all these people.

'He told police invaluable information of the other eight deaths [in which he wasn't involved]. He refined police inquiries and the evidence uncovered subsequently proves the truth of his first interview.

'There was a promise of consideration of immunity in the first interview, even though he admitted murder. At that point [June 1999] he was arrested and charged with the murder of David Johnson. It was not until April 2000 that he was told he would not be receiving immunity.

'James Vlassakis was the only one of the accused to submit to the identification line-up process.

'The identification of the deceased was one of the most valuable pieces of information provided. For all of them it was not necessarily known. That was the lynchpin that allowed police to focus their inquiries to match property – he told police of cars and items taken from the victims. He told of the tape recordings and the tape recording of Elizabeth Haydon was found in John Bunting's possession, the computer voice recording. He produced items of evidence to the police, credit cards et cetera.

'He presented a PIN number and receipt from David Johnson. He said Wagner had stored David Johnson's PIN number in his phone and, when the phone was seized, there it was.'

Vlassakis also told police of how – at Bunting's

instigation – he had posed as Fred Brooks on visits to a doctor to try to obtain an alternative social security benefit.

'He told police of the existence of the two bodies at 203 Waterloo Corner Road. James Vlassakis told police about the "U-Store-It" facility which was very important to provide evidence linking John Bunting to the death of Ray Davies. James Vlassakis told police of the source of the barrels. There are literally probably hundreds of pieces of evidence but there's a broad sample of the sorts of matters brought forward by my client.

'John Bunting instructed James Vlassakis at his arrest to get rid of the things in the cars. James Vlassakis didn't do that. He never attempted to do that. He did not come forward as a result of police approaching him; he went to police.

'Before he pleaded, he offered to assist police and prosecuting authorities. In September 2000 he participated in the lengthy second interview.

'James Vlassakis became upset from time to time but generally speaking was much more composed. He will continue to cooperate in any way that's reasonably requested and will participate in any further interviews requested of him.

'There's shown an inherent underlying consistency between the two interviews. The main difference is the reference to the role of Elizabeth Harvey.

'It's probably fair to say that the DPP always believed Elizabeth Harvey had a direct role in the murders. It was probably not a surprise. There were long discussions in regard to immunity and it was only late in 2000 that her interviews were disclosed because of problems about her wanting more extensive immunity.'

As she argued for leniency for her client, Rosemary Davey drew on the opinion of two psychiatrists. The court was told that James Vlassakis was a young man profoundly affected by his disturbed childhood. His mother had suffered from significant psychiatric disorders and a very disturbed personality. She would have found it very difficult to provide any consistent or effective care to her children, and this led to a disruptive life for the children.

For Vlassakis there was no consistent care and no kind of parental model that might have given some fortitude and stability to his character. He was left with very little strength of character, vulnerable because of the severe sexual abuse in his past and the absence of any supportive male figure in his life. There was no close or ongoing relationship with anyone, other than his disordered relationship with his mother.

Sexual abuse, in the context of Vlassakis's already disturbed background, was even more damaging than it might otherwise have been. There was abuse as a young child and in early adolescence, and on both occasions he may well have been exposed to the grossest forms of sexual abuse. To an already damaged and vulnerable youth, this was devastating to his development.

As a result of all this, James Vlassakis developed a long-standing depression.

Depressed people are easily caught up and suborned by others because they desperately seek support and comfort during depression. They are also susceptible to drug use.

The court heard that one psychiatrist was struck by the way in which Vlassakis was greatly drawn into John Bunting's world. First he was pulled into the peculiar set of beliefs that John Bunting had about paedophiles, the threat of paedophiles, his 'missions' to save children from paedophiles. At the same time Vlassakis became involved in the behaviour: property damage, then theft and violence.

Bunting introduced him to guns as well, then shooting and the killing and torture of animals.

This was a kind of grooming, a gradual introduction to escalating criminal behaviour and into the world and thinking of John Bunting.

The same psychiatrist noted that serial killings are fortunately rare. Serial killings involving more than one person are extremely rare. Such a terrible set of undertakings rarely occurs with a group of people agreeing to involve themselves in such behaviour; it also requires that the people have a remarkable level of trust in each other. Largely they are people driven by perverse sexual motivations; the vast majority are essentially sadistic. For a group to be involved it needs to be a group that either shares that sadistic drive or has somehow been persuaded to assist someone in gratifying their perverse needs.

John Bunting had been totally preoccupied with the notion of a conspiracy of paedophiles – a network of paedophiles – and preoccupied with the notion that somehow he had a role to save or protect children, firstly by exposing paedophiles, later by killing them. He appears to have been constantly preoccupied with these themes and to have drawn others into his preoccupations.

Without examining Bunting, one expert said he couldn't tell whether he had a peculiar set of beliefs which had arisen out of his experiences in real life, or whether they stemmed from a paranoid illness. On the face of it Bunting was profoundly disturbed, and the question was why and how he used that disturbance to justify the most horrific of acts. Clearly there were other elements that came into the dreadful mixture which led to these crimes, but paedophilia provided the superficial justification for his actions.

The expert believed that John Bunting could be

psychotic, but possibly not psychopathic – although on the material available he might be both.

The psychiatrists believed James Vlassakis was not psychopathic. The evidence of this was the young man's distress and difficulty in recounting the torture and murders. This was not someone who had taken pleasure in the victims' suffering. Vlassakis was not calm, calculating and collected; instead he was as overwhelmed as any normal person would be by the horror of such acts as they had participated in.

The relationship between John Bunting and James Vlassakis was more than dependent: James was totally dominated by John Bunting. He had become caught up in the abnormal world of John Bunting and it was only with the passage of many months that he had been able to separate himself from John Bunting. So this was not just admiring someone or accepting their views; it was a matter of feeling almost completely under the control and influence of someone else, so that he came to accept his bizarre and twisted views of the world as the natural and real world in which they lived.

The expert conclusion was that Vlassakis could mature and develop – one day emerging as a man who was not anti-social, damaged or vicious.

These sentiments were echoed by Ms Davey as she concluded her impassioned plea for her client to be given a glimpse of freedom, albeit decades away.

'My client is kept in a very restrictive regime. The consequence to him of his incarceration for the foreseeable future is that he welcomes few visitors. He has recently had the support of a nun and another supportive visitor.

'He has commenced further education. He is studying his Year 11 and 12 simultaneously. He has presently indicated great interest in commencing a course through the TAFE polytechnic, which he hopes to do.

'My client has publicly acknowledged his legal and moral responsibility for these deaths. He, at twenty-one, had the courage, the moral fortitude, to face up to his responsibility. Although he did not physically kill, he knows he is both morally and legally a murderer.

'This court and community should recognise the courage of this young man and the progress and maturity he has shown.

'The persons who should have protected my client failed to do so. Elizabeth Harvey left her son in the care of a man she knew to be a callous and wicked killer. John Bunting did nothing but initiate my client into a world of evil and malignancy.

'He [Vlassakis] will spend a long time in prison. He knows that, he accepts that and he feels that he deserves it. But we say on his behalf that James Vlassakis has never had a life. He has never had any joy, any family. He is truly alone. He will not marry nor have children. He is denied his freedom and that is the way it must be. But he is not evil. He has participated in evil but he is also worthy of redemption. We ask for the mercy of this court. Because it's right that although he be punished, he be shown mercy too.'

Late in his sentencing submissions hearing, James Vlassakis opted to speak for himself. Dressed in a white shirt, red patterned tie and blue slacks, the then twenty-one year old stood in the dock flanked by Ms Davey and a court sheriff. He fought back tears as he read from a written statement. It was as much an apology as it was a plea for mercy.

'I would like to begin by thanking Your Honour for giving me a chance to say how sorry I am to the people who I've caused so much pain and suffering to. As I look back and reflect on the past I wonder what went wrong and why I cannot change these terrible things I have done. If only I could change the past. I know that nothing I can ever say will justify the terrible way these people were viciously murdered and no one could ever deserve what happened to them.

'I hope one day I can forgive myself for what I have done. At this point in time I can never do this. I hate myself for the fact that I have done this. I have to live with the pain and suffering I have caused the victims' family and friends. It sickens me to think that I have been involved in taking away precious lives from their loved ones. When I lie in bed at night I think I don't know myself any more and I try to come to terms with what I have done. In the mornings I wake up and I think, why? How could I do this? When I look in the mirror and look at my face I think it's not me. How did I end up in this position? These questions I cannot answer but in time hopefully I can. I could kill myself tomorrow and then I think this would be the easy way out. The choices I've made will affect my life forever.

'I can only hope by pleading guilty and giving evidence in the trial to come I can offer a little peace to the family and friends of the victims, by owning up to my mistakes and admitting my guilt to myself, society, families, relatives and friends. Because I have taken away a loved one, a part of someone's life, and changed everyone's lives forever. Now is the time to face up to my mistakes and own up to my responsibilities for the actions I have taken. I am so sorry for what I have done and could never forgive myself. I offer my sincere and unconditional sorrow for the pain I have caused to the families, friends and relatives. I know that neither what I have said today nor anything else will ever make up for the pain I have caused. I know the suffering you have experienced and I know that you can never forgive me, but I am sorry.'

Prosecutor Wendy Abraham conceded there was no opposition to the setting of a non-parole period for James Vlassakis. Nonetheless, she argued for a significantly lengthy jail term.

'When one looks at these murders, what one is talking about is premeditated, cold-blooded and extensive torture. The men took property and accessed social security.

'There is no comparable case.

'Ordinarily, being involved in a number of murders of this type would result in fixing life imprisonment with no non-parole period. The Crown accepts the accused is entitled to substantial credit as a result of pleading guilty and cooperation with the authorities. The Crown says that could amount to exceptional circumstances, justifying a non-parole period where ordinarily one would not be fixed.

'There has been a lot made of the cooperation with the authorities. Not everything put about the value of his second interview is necessarily accepted.

'It's correct that as a result of the decision to call James Vlassakis there are two extra charges. But there was physical evidence: DNA, handwriting, fingerprints, family members, social security records, and police knew about the "U-Store-It", property in the houses.

'The Crown only concedes that he expedited inquiries.

'Of course, what the Crown didn't have was an eyewitness account, and we accept that.

'In this state, the worst category of murder should receive twenty-five to thirty-five years just for one.

'Listening to Mr Vlassakis this morning it's very easy to have some sympathy for him. But we are talking about four of the most horrific murders one could imagine. Don't overlook punitive factors. His role was very important. He got them into various places. Those murders would not have occurred at that time without him. He provided John Bunting with information about whether Gary O'Dwyer was on a pension before the murder. A younger person was needed to impersonate Fred Brooks. It's simply not right to say he was not essential simply because his role was not as violent as the others'.

'He was still clearly capable of making a choice.'

Justice Duggan passed sentence a little under a month later:

'If it had not been for your plea of guilty, your extensive cooperation with the police and your undertaking to give evidence for the prosecution ... I would have imposed a non-parole period of forty-two years.

'However, it is an acknowledged sentencing principle that quite significant reductions in sentence are given to those who not only plead guilty but also assist the police in their investigations and who undertake to give evidence against alleged co-offenders.

'I am satisfied that you have given extensive assistance to the police in this matter and I take into account your undertaking to give evidence. Your confinement is likely to be much more restrictive than would otherwise be the case. There is an element of remorse apparent in your conduct since you were arrested on these charges.

'I fix a non-parole period of twenty-six years to date from 2 June 1999, the date when you were taken into custody.

'The effect of the non-parole period is that parole cannot be granted until the period of twenty-six years is served. After that, it is up to the authorities as to whether and when you will be released.'

TWENTY-FOUR

James Vlassakis had confessed to his role in the serial killings, turned star witness and thrown himself on the mercy of the court. He hoped one day to be a free man. John Bunting, Robert Wagner and Mark Haydon instructed their legal teams to fight on, even in the face of the damning eyewitness testimony Vlassakis would inevitably deliver.

On 13 August 2001, Bunting, Wagner and Haydon stood in a South Australian Supreme Court dock to officially plead not guilty to ten counts of murder – those of Ray Davies, Suzanne Allen, Michael Gardiner, Barry Lane, Gavin Porter, Troy Youde, Fred Brooks, Gary O'Dwyer, Elizabeth Haydon and David Johnson.

The sheer magnitude of the case meant pre-trial argument did not begin until March 2002, and by then prosecutors had dealt another blow. Bunting and Haydon were charged with a further two counts of murder over the deaths of Clinton Trezise in 1992 and Thomas Trevilyan in 1997. Wagner was also charged with Trevilyan's murder, and with assisting an offender in relation to Trezise's killing. The trio pleaded not guilty to the additional charges in February 2002. The number of alleged murders was now twelve – unprecedented in Australian criminal history.

However, prosecutors would not have it all their own

way. As evidence was examined and contested during the pre-trial process, it became clear that the case against Mark Haydon was, in some respects, weak. It appeared Haydon had been on the fringes of activity as John Bunting and Robert Wagner had embarked on their murder spree. The prosecutors did argue that Haydon not only had direct involvement in killing his wife and Troy Youde, but also helped hide victims' bodies and cover the killers' tracks. They said he should be tried and convicted of all twelve murders because he took part in a 'joint enterprise'. The trial judge disagreed. Justice Brian Martin ruled that the evidence wasn't sufficient for Haydon to stand trial on nine of the twelve murder counts, leaving only those of Elizabeth Haydon, Troy Youde and Clinton Trezise. It was later decided that the Trezise count would also be dropped.

Haydon's legal team – headed by prominent defence barrister Marie Shaw QC – also won the right for their client to stand trial separately to Bunting and Wagner. After much deliberation it was deemed Haydon would go to trial after his co-accused, charged only with the murders of Troy Youde and Elizabeth Haydon. In addition prosecutors elected to pursue him on six counts of assisting offenders, the charges relating to the other victims whose bodies were stored in barrels in the old Snowtown bank vault. The prosecutors were certain Haydon had played a vital role in concealing and moving the barrels while also profiting from the murders.

Perhaps Mrs Shaw was pushing her client's luck when she asked that Haydon be released on bail while he awaited trial, saying, 'We understand he has been a model remandee. Our main concern is our client had been in custody for three years.'

Not surprisingly, bail was refused.

Bunting and Wagner were now slated to stand trial together, in the biggest serial killing case the nation had ever seen. All along the pair had protested their innocence, instructing their lawyers to contest virtually every shred of evidence, to argue at every turn. To some it seemed that Bunting and Wagner were revelling in the process, basking in the spotlight and enjoying the fight. So it was a stunning move when, two weeks before the trial opening, Robert Wagner stood in court and admitted guilt.

On 27 September 2002, Wagner pleaded guilty to three of the murder charges: Barry Lane, Fred Brooks and David Johnson. He maintained his innocence on the remaining counts and showed no signs of cooperating with police. Wagner was still very much at John Bunting's side.

After almost four years of legal wrangling, and more than a thousand witness statements, the trial of John Bunting and Robert Wagner began on 16 October 2002. It was to be staged in a courtroom refurbished at a cost of $3 million – modified and enlarged to accommodate the sheer volume of jurors, lawyers, evidence and spectators. Computer monitors were installed so photographs of evidence could be displayed electronically. The whole of South Australia steeled itself for the true horrors of this case to be revealed in open court – and to the public – for the first time.

The jury consisted of fifteen members – more than the usual twelve, in anticipation that some may find the case too horrific to endure. The previous day there had been a false start to the trial when a juror begged to be excused, explaining that the details were too distressing to hear.

A hush fell over the custom-built courtroom as Wendy Abraham QC rose to her feet before Justice Brian Martin and the jury. The public gallery was full, with media seated closest to the front, then victims' families and police who had worked the case. There was also a scattering of curious members of the public. As Ms Abraham began to speak there was absolute silence. Her presence and her words commanded attention – and she had it.

'On the 20th of May 1999, when the police opened the vault of the disused State Bank at Snowtown, they were met with a pungent smell of rotting or decomposing meat.

'What they found inside was shocking. There were barrels containing rotting human remains, knives, handcuffs, gloves – items used in the murder, torture and mutilation of bodies.

'There were eight bodies in six barrels. In the following days, a further two bodies were found buried in the back yard of a Salisbury North house.'

With poise and precision Ms Abraham would spend the next two days delivering her opening address, decisively pointing to the guilt of John Bunting and Robert Wagner, who watched and listened from behind a glass barrier only a few metres away. Ms Abraham detailed the mountain of evidence against not only Bunting and Wagner, but also Vlassakis – now her prize witness – and Haydon, who would face trial later.

'The Crown says each of these deaths was part of a series of murders committed by the accused. Some time later two further deaths were linked to this series.

'As members of the community your initial reaction may well have been one of horror. Horror at what had been found and indeed that it happened in our community.

'You have now been called upon to represent that community to decide issues in this trial. You therefore have to put aside any initial reactions you felt, you must distance yourself and evaluate the evidence you hear in this courtroom.

'What the Crown alleges the accused did in committing

these crimes can only be described as horrific. The mere reciting of some of the allegations is indeed shocking.

'I have a duty to adduce the evidence to you. I make no apologies for making the allegations, nor for leading the evidence. What you will hear and see at times will be very unpleasant and distasteful to say the least. The description of some of the events will be chilling. However, the Crown must prove its case and this is what the Crown says they did.

'The events you will hear about began in 1992.

'It's alleged that in 1992 the accused Bunting murdered Clinton Trezise. Robert Wagner helped him to dispose of his body.

'Thereafter it's alleged between December 1995 and May 1999 John Bunting and Robert Wagner together murdered eleven people ... You will hear that in some of these murders the accused tortured their victims, that they obtained information from them so they could claim their Centrelink benefits after they were murdered. They took their property. They would tell stories to explain their disappearance. They would impersonate their victims where necessary.

'The bodies of some of the victims were dismembered and some defleshed.

'You will hear that the accused bragged, boasted and laughed about what they had done.

'There's evidence of some of these features in at least ten of these murders. Those of Ray Davies, Suzanne Allen, Michael Gardiner, Barry Lane, Gavin Porter, Troy Youde, Fred Brooks, Gary O'Dwyer, Elizabeth Haydon and David Johnson.

'The Crown says that the evidence will reveal there was a system or pattern for the commission of these murders that the accused developed and refined over time.

'The Crown says that the murder of Thomas Trevilyan,

although it does not have those features, is nevertheless linked to the series. It's alleged that as the murders progressed, the patterns to the murders included murdering people who had knowledge of a previous murder and posed a risk to the accused. You will hear that Thomas Trevilyan, Barry Lane and Elizabeth Haydon had such knowledge.

'Consequently the Crown says that the evidence will demonstrate there's an underlying unity between all of these murders, so much so that from the time of the murder of Ray Davies, the accused were, in effect, in the business of killing.'

Next Ms Abraham guided the jurors through the police investigation into Elizabeth Haydon's disappearance and how it led to the discovery of the remains at Snowtown. How, in the weeks before, the barrels had been hurriedly shifted from Mark Haydon's garage to a property rented by friends of Bunting and Wagner. Finally, the remains had been secreted in the old bank vault.

'It is the Crown case that John Bunting and Mark Haydon rented the bank in 1999. In January 1999 the then owners of the bank, Rosemary and Andrew Michael, were approached by two men to rent the property. They met with these two men, who introduced themselves as John and Mark. The men were shown through the bank and an agreement was reached to rent it. A key was provided to them.

'On February 8, 1999 the Michaels left a rental agreement and a rent book in the bank to be completed by those renting it. On February 10 the agreement, which had been completed in handwriting, was left at the post office, with the rent money, in the name of John Bunting and Mark Lawrence of 4 Blackham Crescent, Smithfield Plains. Lawrence was Mark Haydon's name before he married Elizabeth Haydon.

'The handwriting on the rental agreement was examined by Sharon Birchall [an expert on handwriting], who compared the writing and signatures with the known writing of John Bunting and Mark Haydon. Having done so, she formed the opinion that there were similarities and no significant differences between the handwriting on the document and that of John Bunting, similarly with his signature. She is also of the opinion that there are similarities between the signature of Mark Lawrence and the known signatures of Mark Haydon. John Bunting's thumbprint is on the document.

'Rosemary and Andrew Michael were separately shown a number of photographs by the police. Each of them identified a photograph of John Bunting as one of the persons involved in the transaction. Andrew Michael also identified a photograph of Mark Haydon. Rosemary Michael said she was 70 per cent sure she had seen Robert Wagner at the Snowtown post office. Arrangements had been made for the rent for the bank to be paid at that post office.

'Naturally a key was provided to the bank as part of the rental agreement, but no key was provided to the vault. John Bunting and Robert Wagner wanted to be able to lock the vault, so Simon Jones assisted them in fashioning a piece of wire to be used as a key. It's alleged at some time thereafter they moved the contents of the Land Cruiser to the bank and stored the barrels in the vault.

'After that time, John Bunting, Robert Wagner, Mark Haydon and James Vlassakis were seen to visit Snowtown and indeed the bank. At times, each was observed going in and out of the vault. On occasions they were observed to be wearing overalls and gloves. On some occasions they would go to the Joneses' to have a shower and change their clothes because they would smell. They would tell the Joneses a story about what they had been doing.'

The jury was told of the forensic process through which

the eight bodies in the barrels were identified: fingerprints, DNA, X-rays. They were Michael Gardiner, Barry Lane, Gavin Porter, Troy Youde, Fred Brooks, Gary O'Dwyer, Elizabeth Haydon and David Johnson.

Ms Abraham alleged there were other murder victims too: the skeleton found at Lower Light later identified as Clinton Trezise; Thomas Trevilyan, found hanged from a tree; and Ray Davies and Suzanne Allen, who had been buried in the back yard of Bunting's former home.

'A postmortem examination was conducted in relation to each of the victims. Given the condition of many of the bodies, the pathologists were not able to determine a cause of death for many of the victims. However, in relation to five of the victims, the probable cause of death was strangulation or asphyxiation. They were Michael Gardiner, Barry Lane, Troy Youde, Fred Brooks and Elizabeth Haydon.

'One of the victims was hung by a rope, that being Trevilyan. One died as a result of multiple blows with a blunt object to the back of his head, that's Clinton Trezise.

'Four of the victims in the barrels were found with gags in their mouths, for example a sock, with the gags securely fastened with tape around their mouth and head. They were Lane, Youde, Brooks and Haydon.

'Four of the victims still had a rope tied around their necks. Gardiner, Lane, Youde and Haydon.

'Those with electrical cord or rope around their legs were Fred Brooks and Elizabeth Haydon.

'Rope was found in two of the bags with the remains of Suzanne Allen.

'Fred Brooks had his hands handcuffed behind his back and his legs tied together.

'Gary O'Dwyer had marks on his chest suggestive of electrical burns.

'A number of the victims' bodies had been dismembered, with their legs or feet removed from the bodies or their bodies cut up. They were Suzanne Allen, Michael Gardiner, Troy Youde, Barry Lane and David Johnson.

'With Troy Youde and Suzanne Allen, not only had their bodies been dismembered, but some of the bones had all the skin and muscle cut off them. They were defleshed. The condition of the bodies was such that other injuries suffered by them could easily have been obscured or marked. The pathologists cannot exclude that other things were inflicted upon them, because of the condition of the bodies.

'It's alleged that within the bank or the vault were paraphernalia or instruments associated with the torture, murder and later mutilation of the victims.

'The condition of the victims' bodies, the results of the postmortem examinations, together with the items in the bank, give us some insight as to what the victims had been subjected to before and after their murders.

'The implements and other items associated with the murders found in the vault included knives. There were seven knives in a plastic tray on the top of an upended lounge in the vault. Two knives were on top of barrel B, one was stained. There was one on top of barrel A.

'There were handcuffs on top of barrel A.

'Gloves. There was a large number of used or soiled gloves. Within the vault there were over ninety-three used gloves as well as boxes of unused gloves.

'There was adhesive tape that was stained which had hair stuck on it. There was a piece of rope that was knotted with hair caught in the knot. There were sparklers, both new and used.

'There was a machine called a Variac machine, capable of inflicting electric shocks.

'There was property belonging to David Johnson, Troy Youde and Fred Brooks, including David Johnson's wallet and a notebook in which the Crown alleges in John Bunting's handwriting was David Johnson's PIN and names and phrases.

'The Crown says this list in itself is very telling. These items were taken to the forensic science centre. A number were taken for DNA analysis.

'DNA profiles were done on the accused at the time of their arrests. No DNA was able to be obtained from the victims because of the condition of their bodies in this case. DNA was obtained from the parents to determine the likely profile of the child. That was not able to be done for all of the victims.

'They tested the knives on top of barrel B, together with two rubber gloves, and on one of the knives were stains. The stains had a DNA typing consistent with David Johnson. On one of the gloves was a piece of muscle. This had a DNA typing consistent with David Johnson. Part of David Johnson's thigh had been cut away.

'On the vault floor was brown packing adhesive tape with hair on it. It had a DNA type consistent with that of David Johnson. Swabs from the tape again revealed a DNA type consistent with David Johnson.

'There were a number of garbage bags in the vault. With these were a large number of used and soiled gloves. Three of those gloves had DNA typing consistent with John Bunting.

'Sixteen samples from thirteen gloves were consistent with the DNA typing of Robert Wagner. On two of those gloves, the DNA was consistent with Robert Wagner on the inner and outer surface.

'There was DNA consistent with Mark Haydon on six gloves.

'It's alleged they were worn by the accused whilst bodies were being handled.

'Also, seven samples from five gloves were consistent with Troy Youde.

'Three samples from two gloves were consistent with David Johnson.

'One glove was consistent with Troy Youde on the outside and John Bunting on the inside.

'There was a piece of rope with hair caught in the knot. A stain on the rope and the hair was consistent with Troy Youde.

'Rope on the bank counter with stains on it was consistent with Gavin Porter.

'There were sparklers, new and used. It's alleged the sparklers were used in the torture of at least one of the victims. Eight of the gloves tested had barium, the principal component of sparklers. One of these gloves also had the DNA typing of Robert Wagner.

'Some items were found within the bank, for example, the knives, handcuffs, Variac machine; in addition there are some items of the same or similar nature found in the homes and or vehicles of the accused. Handcuff keys, sparklers, gloves, tape, rope. You will also hear of items located in the accused's homes and or vehicles which the Crown says were generated or created in the course of committing the murders. For example, pieces of paper with the personal details of the victim recorded on them.'

With the help of photographs and a chart, the jury was shown the links between all of the accused and their victims. Five victims had been living with one of the accused at the time of their murders. Four victims were related to one of their killers.

Then, Ms Abraham told the jurors, there was the web of deceit created by the killers to cover up their crimes.

'It's alleged that the accused between them would create and spread false stories about their victims ... to explain their absence to family and friends. Where necessary, the accused between them created the impression that the victims were alive and their disappearance was in some way explicable. These victims were Ray Davies, Suzanne Allen, Michael Gardiner, Barry Lane, Thomas Trevilyan, Gavin Porter, Troy Youde, Fred Brooks, Gary O'Dywer, Elizabeth Haydon and David Johnson.

'What was needed to be done depended on the circumstances. Some of the victims chosen appear to have had little contact with family and few friends. Some were never reported as missing persons. However, it's alleged when a situation did arise where an explanation was required, they told false stories. These stories included, on some occasions, stories to the police who had become involved in missing persons inquiries. Generally they included stories that the victim was alive and had chosen to leave or that they had seen a victim after a time they had been murdered. In at least one murder there's evidence a victim was told to make phone calls to family members before they were killed.

'As the murders progressed and the accused became more sophisticated, they began making recordings of the voices of their victims. On at least three occasions, words or phrases were recorded, initially on a tape recorder but on the last occasion on computer.'

Police recovered voice recordings of five victims. The most recent, of David Johnson, was found on the hard drive of John Bunting's computer. The series of statements was recorded in the old Snowtown bank on the night of his murder.

On the day of Bunting's arrest an audiocassette was

discovered in the ceiling of his home. It had been hastily hidden in a sock which had been stuffed into a shoe. The tape contained statements Elizabeth Haydon had been forced to yell in the minutes before she was killed, calling her mother a 'whore' and telling her children to 'die'.

'Mum, did you tell the women at the church you are a whore? If you ever ring again I'm going to tell every fuckhead at the church you are a whore.'

A second audiotape was handed to police by Robert Wagner's fiancée, Sally Brown. She had discovered it in their home more than a year after his arrest. It contained the voices of Troy Youde, Fred Brooks and Gary O'Dwyer. Again there was a series of abusive statements directed towards family and friends. In each voice is a measure of confusion and fear – by this time the victims may have sensed they were to be killed. During one sickening portion of the Gary O'Dwyer recording, he is asked by Bunting if he was in pain during his torture. 'Yes,' Gary replied, 'it did hurt lots.'

As she delivered her case outline, Wendy Abraham explained to the jury that the recordings were made so they could be played over the telephone to victims' families or friends, creating the impression they were still alive.

'It's alleged that the purpose behind these recordings was to ensure that the disappearance of these victims would not be reported to authorities, or to divert attention away from the accused.

'It's alleged that property identified as belonging to the victims or property in a victim's name was located after the arrest of an accused when police searched their homes, vehicles and other premises associated with them. The addresses you will mainly hear about are where the accused were living at the time of their arrests.

'At each of these addresses were a number of vehicles and property was also located in a number of those vehicles.'

Ms Abraham told the jury that victims' property had also been found in a storage unit, rented by John Bunting from a company named U-Store-It.

'The evidence in this category can be divided into two. First there's the property owned by a victim or in the name of a victim which was in existence at the time of their murder. And, secondly, that generated after the murder.

'Police found property in premises associated with the accused in relation to eleven of the twelve victims.

'John Bunting had property belonging to Ray Davies, Suzanne Allen, Michael Gardiner, Barry Lane, Thomas Trevilyan, Gavin Porter, Troy Youde, Fred Brooks, Gary O'Dwyer and David Johnson.

'Robert Wagner had property belonging to Ray Davies, Suzanne Allen, Michael Gardiner, Barry Lane, Gavin Porter, Fred Brooks, Gary O'Dwyer, Elizabeth Haydon and David Johnson.

'There's also evidence of property being in their possession at an earlier point in time but being disposed of prior to their arrests.

'There were cars, large items of furniture including a lounge, televisions, refrigerators, financial documentation, keycards and bank books.

'Often the property of a number of victims was stored together. In the ceiling of Bundarra Court was the property of the victims Suzanne Allen, Barry Lane, Gavin Porter, Troy Youde, Fred Brooks, Thomas Trevilyan. Much of this was documentation kept in several bags, for example one bag contained the property of five victims. Also in the bag was a wallet with the property of four victims. Also in the ceiling, for example, the tape recording of Elizabeth Haydon's voice, and documents recording information the Crown says was obtained from the victims before their murders. There were practice signatures for Gavin Porter, Troy Youde and Gary O'Dwyer. In Robert Wagner's car, the blue Ford Marquis SMX 289, there were items belonging to Ray Davies, Michael Gardiner, Barry Lane, Gavin Porter, Fred Brooks and Gary O'Dwyer. In that vehicle there was a bumbag. In the bumbag there were four separate wallets containing cards and financial documentation relating to victims. It will be apparent that with some of the victims, both accused had property of those victims in their vehicles. Mark Haydon also had property of eight victims in his home or vehicles.

'The accused between them continued to claim the victims' Centrelink benefits. Those of Ray Davies, Suzanne Allen, Barry Lane, Gavin Porter, Troy Youde, Fred Brooks Gary O'Dwyer and David Johnson.

'It's alleged they were able to do this because before the murder they would obtain the necessary information from them. Then after the murder they would take documentation from the victims' homes. The types of information they would obtain from their victims included PINs, bank details, but also personal information including previous addresses and relatives' names. The amount of information depended on how well they knew the victim.

'Documents alleged to have been obtained before the murders include those belonging to Suzanne Allen, Gavin Porter, Fred Brooks, Gary O'Dwyer and David Johnson. Pieces of paper were found recording the details of Suzanne Allen, Gavin Porter, Fred Brooks, Gary O'Dwyer at Bunting's home. Johnson's details were found in Robert Wagner's phone.

'It's alleged between them they took whatever steps were necessary to ensure a victim's benefits continued to be paid into that victim's account. That included filling out forms, attending appointments, notifying of a change of address, re-establishing a victim's benefits if for some reason Centrelink stopped paying, setting up a bank account in a victim's name.'

It was John Bunting who would orchestrate the theft of money from victims' bank accounts after their murders, taking whatever steps necessary to ensure their government welfare payments continued to be paid. It was a brazen, but not clever, move. The siphoning of cash continued undetected only because victims had not been reported missing or their disappearances were not considered suspicious, in many cases because of the illusions created by the killers themselves. On occasions Bunting and his accomplices would impersonate victims to ensure their flow of funds was not halted. Bunting sent letters and submitted bank or government forms in the names of his victims, even impersonating at least one – Ray Davies – on the telephone and in person. Where he could not pose as a victim himself, he enlisted the help of others.

However, the charades left behind a mountain of evidence which contributed in no small part to the case against the killers. Typical of this was the impersonation of Fred Brooks. While it was James Vlassakis who was given the task of impersonating Fred Brooks, the deception was directed by Bunting. At the time of his murder Brooks had been receiving the fortnightly welfare payment appropriate for a young man studying and living at home. When Brooks was dead and the killers were stealing his money, they wanted more, so Bunting hatched a plan to change the benefit to a more substantial rate paid to homeless people. Bunting wanted to depict the so-called Fred Brooks as mentally ill and, as a result, homeless and unable to work.

In September 1998 – only days after Fred Brooks's murder – Vlassakis posed as Brooks during a doctor's visit. With him was John Bunting, using the alias Gavin Allen (the Christian names of Gavin Porter). The visit was to obtain a medical certificate. Six days later the pair attended a Centrelink office and submitted several forms and the medical certificate in an effort to change the address for 'Fred Brooks' and boost his benefit. To be approved for the more substantial benefit, Vlassakis, again posing as Fred Brooks, attended appointments with a Centrelink social worker, and during the third appointment Bunting and Wagner also went along. Some time later Brooks's payment was suspended because the required fortnightly forms were not submitted. Again an impersonation was undertaken, with Vlassakis posing as Brooks on the telephone, then in person to explain he had not lodged his forms because he was schizophrenic. This excuse required yet another medical certificate, which prompted a series of further doctor's visits. During one, Vlassakis gave a blood sample.

While the killers succeeded in getting more money, they also left behind a trail of evidence. Both the social worker and doctor later identified James Vlassakis as 'Fred Brooks' and John Bunting as his friend, 'Gavin Allen'. Robert Wagner was identified as having accompanied them during one appointment. Vlassakis's fingerprint was found on a document supposedly filled out by 'Fred Brooks' and the blood sample was matched by DNA to Vlassakis.

In order to claim Suzanne Allen's money, Bunting had his de facto wife, Elizabeth Harvey, and, later, his unwitting fiancée, Gail Sinclair, pose as Allen. They would assume her identity during telephone calls, to obtain post office boxes and even open new bank accounts. A large quantity of paperwork in Suzanne Allen's name was found in Gail Sinclair's briefcase at the time the killers were arrested. Similar documents were found in Elizabeth Harvey's handbag.

This evidence, Wendy Abraham told the jury, was compelling.

'In the case of seven of the eight victims where Centrelink benefits were claimed, the accused had documentation in relation to a Centrelink claim. The only one where they didn't was with David Johnson. They were arrested less than two weeks after his murder. The documentation in relation to some victims was found with more than one accused.

'In the case of each victim, the accused between them made regular withdrawals from the accounts up until the time of their arrests.

'The access or keycards for those accounts were located in the accused's homes or vehicles or provided to police by James Vlassakis. There were even two cards located for two of the victims whose benefits they were unable to access. There's evidence from the banking records as to when, where and how much money was withdrawn from accounts. These records also reveal a pattern as to where withdrawals were made from some of the victims' accounts. For example, withdrawals from their accounts after the murders occurred in different locations from before they were murdered. In relation to Ray Davies and Suzanne Allen, withdrawals were made at Murray Bridge when John Bunting was living at Murray Bridge. Withdrawals from six victims' accounts were made from the ATM at the BP Express at Munno Para. Withdrawals from five accounts were from the Mobil Quix at Hillbank. At the BP Munno Para there were also withdrawals from John Bunting and Mark Haydon's account. At the Mobil there were withdrawals from Robert Wagner's account.

'It's alleged in relation to Ray Davies and Suzanne Allen there are video recordings of John Bunting withdrawing money from their accounts. In relation to Barry Lane, there's video of Robert Wagner accessing his account.

'The total amount obtained from Centrelink was nearly $95 000.'

As they pilfered the bank accounts of eight of their victims, the killers incriminated themselves time and time again. In every case evidence was found linking the accused to transactions on the victims' accounts. This was the summary presented to the jury:

Ray Davies: His welfare benefits were paid into an account with the Australian Central Credit Union, the card for which was found at Bunting's house. Security cameras at three Credit Union branches recorded images of a person posing as Ray Davies to withdraw money from his account. There were six recordings; on each occasion it was John Bunting in the video.

Suzanne Allen: Payments also into an Australian Central Credit Union account. Card also found at Bunting's house. In December 1998, at Bunting's request, [Gail Sinclair] opened another account at the Savings and Loans Credit Union in Suzanne Allen's name. Allen's Centrelink benefits were subsequently paid into this account.

In February 1999 a security camera recorded a person withdrawing money from Suzanne Allen's bank account. The withdrawals were made from an ATM at a BP Express service station in the northern Adelaide suburb of Munno Para. The person shown in the video is John Bunting.

Barry Lane: Welfare benefits paid into his Bank of South Australia account. Card for this account was discovered at Robert Wagner's house. In July 1998 a surveillance camera was installed by police at an ATM at the BP Express service station at Elizabeth Grove, in Adelaide's northern suburbs. It filmed Robert Wagner making withdrawals from Barry Lane's account. Four months later Wagner was watched by undercover police as he made another withdrawal. Between November 1998 and February 1999 a security camera filmed Wagner making another four such withdrawals. Receipts for these transactions were retrieved by police from a nearby rubbish bin – two had Wagner's fingerprints on them. In April and May 1999 a camera at the BP Express, Munno Para, filmed Wagner making another three withdrawals from Lane's account.

Gavin Porter: Commonwealth Bank account. His card was never found, but a photocopy of the back of this card was discovered in the ceiling of John Bunting's house. Vlassakis confessed to police that Bunting had given him Porter's card to use. Later, Vlassakis said, it was given to Mark Haydon to use. ATM receipts for transactions on this account (made in October 1998) were discovered by police in Haydon's home. Documents relating to this account were found in a car parked at Haydon's house.

Troy Youde: Adelaide Bank account, the card for which was surrendered to police by James Vlassakis. Vlassakis told police Bunting had given him this card to use.

Fred Brooks: Before his murder his welfare benefits were paid into a joint account with his mother, Gail Sinclair. Bunting and Vlassakis diverted the payments into Gavin Porter's account, from which cash was already being stolen. In April 1999 a new account was opened in the name Fred Brooks. Vlassakis opened the account and John Bunting and Mark Haydon were with him. The address given to the bank was Robert Wagner's. Bank documents were discovered with Vlassakis's fingerprints. Vlassakis confessed to police that he had withdrawn cash from this account, and given the money to Mark Haydon, and that Haydon had also made withdrawals himself. Receipts for withdrawals from the Brooks account were found in Haydon's car.

Gary O'Dwyer: Commonwealth Bank account. Card surrendered to police by Vlassakis, who had found it in the home he shared with Bunting. Bunting arranged for the bank to issue a keycard for this account. A signature on the receipt form was matched to Bunting by a handwriting expert.

David Johnson: Bank of South Australia account. Card surrendered to police by Vlassakis. Wagner and Vlassakis unsuccessfully attempted to withdraw cash on the night of Johnson's murder. Vlassakis told police they were able to take out $390 ten days later.

As Wendy Abraham QC stood before them, detailing the plethora of evidence, the jury must already have been forming the view that John Bunting and Robert Wagner were guilty of murder. Ms Abraham was still to address the complex issue of motive.

'It's alleged that John Bunting and Robert Wagner had a hatred for people they characterised as paedophiles. There's evidence that the intensity of feelings on their part was extreme. What's more, there's evidence that can give rise to the inference that John Bunting and Robert Wagner did not distinguish between paedophiles and homosexuals.

'The nature and intensity of their views will be demonstrated by the evidence that they regularly talked about paedophiles and how they should be treated. The intensity of the views is revealed not only in what was said but how it was said and the frequency with which they spoke about this topic.

'It's also demonstrated by the types of material police collected at John Bunting's home and in a U–Store–It container he was renting at the time of his arrest.

'Yellow Post-it notes with names written on them were found. When he was living at 203 Waterloo Corner Road, on the wall of one bedroom of his house he had an item which was referred to as a "spider wall". This consisted of yellow Post-it notes with names written on them stuck to the wall. The individual pieces of paper were linked together by wool. These were the names of people considered to be paedophiles and the names were joined to show links or relationships between people. Parts of this were found in the U–Store–It and the ceiling of his home at Bundarra Court.

'There were also names of people said to be associating with paedophiles and documents alleged to be profiles of particular people and diagrams of links with people and a name in the middle. There were specific references to Barry Lane and Ray Davies.

'There was also a letter written as a poem the Crown alleges was written by Robert Wagner after his arrest. It has the date August 28, 2000 and is signed RJ Wagner. Handwriting analysis has been done and there is a fingerprint on the letter. The Crown alleges that the accused's attitude to paedophiles amongst other things can be inferred from the letter and you will see that in due course.

'The intensity of their attitude towards paedophiles was a common link between them. It was a motive towards committing these crimes.'

The poem was as chilling as it was juvenile. It was sent in letter form to another killer serving his sentence at Yatala Prison. Wagner's literary effort was error-ridden and one mistake stood out above all others: he had misspelled the word paedophile.

I'm a CFS man – my uniform's swank
And I've never been to a Snowtown bank
Yet bodies in barrels – hey I wonder who's there?
Peadophiles [sic] I'm told so who really cares
See so many people are murdered each year
Yet just how many answers can you find around here?
Plus everyone's listening to the media hype
A psychotic killer – hey do I look like the type?
Now in months to come it's my judgement day
You can be sure I'll have my say
And I will not ever be held in contempt
For everyone knows my time was well spent
See you know I only provided a service that's needed
For just like your gardens our street should be weeded
So fuck off Judge Chester in your silly white wig
I only make the streets safe for all of our kids
Now can anyone say what's really what?
For I could be innocent then again maybe not
So fuck all the media and fuck the police
For I know where you live just in case I'm released
Now my poem must end with thoughts of my life
Where did this start – what caused all my strife?
And if my life reads like a Steven [sic] King thriller
You know I'm not a bad guy ...
For a serial killer.

Wendy Abraham continued:

'The Crown is not required to prove a motive for these murders. Evidence which gives rise to a motive by an accused is nevertheless relevant. The Crown says here the evidence will reveal there are a number of common themes underlying why the accused selected the victims they did. For example, their hatred of homosexuals and paedophiles.

'There's evidence from which you can infer that John Bunting and Robert Wagner used this hatred to justify murdering. In relation to some murders there will be no evidence to suggest they exhibited any such behaviour before they were murdered.

'Regardless, it's alleged they were accused during some of the murders of being a "dirty" or a paedophile by the accused.

'Further, there's evidence that at least three of the victims had knowledge of another murder before they were murdered. Those people posed a risk to the accused that they might disclose that information, and so in those circumstances were got rid of. There was also financial gain. Eight victims' benefits. In relation to eleven, they had their property.

'It can be inferred that some of the victims were murdered for a combination of reasons and indeed there might be other reasons.

'Over time, the frequency with which the accused committed these murders increased. The period between the murders got shorter and shorter. Whilst there's a three-year gap between Clinton Trezise and Ray Davies, during the fifteen months thereafter there were eight murders committed. At times there were only weeks between the murders. Of course, with the murder of Elizabeth Haydon the police began making inquiries and there was then a gap of five to six months.

'From the evidence of what the accused did and what they said, you can infer that John Bunting and Robert Wagner enjoyed torturing and murdering their victims. They would laugh, joke, boast and indeed brag about what they had done.'

It took Wendy Abraham two days to outline the case against John Bunting and Robert Wagner. To detail the supporting evidence and hear testimony from 220 Crown witnesses took another 140 days. The testimony of James Vlassakis alone lasted thirty-two days, during which he recounted in sickening detail all he had seen and done, along with much of what he'd been told. The case was compelling; Bunting and Wagner's guilt was proved, it appeared, beyond any shadow of a doubt.

After all this it took the accused men's defence teams a mere eighty minutes to contest the charges. Three witnesses were called by Bunting's lawyers, only one in Wagner's defence.

As the jury was sent to consider its verdicts, Justice Martin directed the jurors to find Robert Wagner not guilty on the charge of assisting to dispose of Clinton Trezise's body. There was, he explained, simply not enough evidence.

For seven days the jurors were locked away from the rest of the world. Father's Day and a round of the AFL football finals passed them by. This group of strangers, called together through no choice of their own, pored once more over the horrific case which had been put to them. Torture, death and deception. For this group of ordinary men and women, the ordeal ended on Monday, 8 September 2003, when a member of the jury knocked on the courtroom door. It was a signal to the court sheriff standing guard outside. They had reached their verdicts.

As anxious legal teams, police and victims' relatives filed back into the courtroom, Bunting and Wagner walked casually in as though the outcome meant little. If they did care, if they were nervous, neither was showing it.

The jury deliberations, however, had not gone

smoothly. The jury forewoman stood and explained to Justice Martin that on one of the murder counts they had not been able to reach a verdict. As to the murder of Suzanne Allen, it was a hung jury. During the trial Bunting and Wagner had claimed Allen died of natural causes, and they had cut her up and disposed of her body. Not all of the jurors had been convinced there was enough evidence to prove otherwise.

As the forewoman read aloud the remaining verdicts, a sense of relief fell over the courtroom. Guilty on all other counts.

Justice Martin thanked the jury with a few telling words: 'With respect to your verdicts, for what it's worth, I agree with you entirely. It's been a long road, hasn't it ... I must say I have nothing but the highest praise for the way each of you have carried out your duties.'

The judge then ordered Bunting and Wagner to stand. One of Bunting's final acts of defiance was to stay seated, but he did have something to say: 'I would have preferred the jury be told the truth about James Vlassakis and the deals he made.'

Justice Martin ordered both men be imprisoned for life – the mandatory sentence for murder in South Australia.

The following month, Bunting and Wagner were again before the court, for Justice Martin to decide if either should have a non-parole period – a time after which they would be eligible for conditional release – set for their sentence. Bunting had ordered his lawyers to say nothing, while Wagner chose to speak for himself. His few sentences gave an insight into the warped mind of a serial killer:

'Paedophiles do terrible things to children and innocent children have been damaged for life. The authorities do nothing about it, I don't know why. I was certainly angry.

Somebody had to do something about it. I decided to take action and I took action. Thank you.'

It was as though Wagner still believed all his victims – most of them innocent and unsuspecting – had deserved to die. There was no hint of remorse, no glimmer of understanding. No trace of reality.

In another pitiful show of contempt, John Bunting sat and read a book as Justice Martin completed the sentencing process. He remarked that the pair had derived pleasure from death and had been in the 'business of killing for pleasure'.

'The evidence given at trial has driven me to the conclusion that both of you are incapable of true rehabilitation.

'The sentence of life with no parole is a dreadful sentence of the utmost severity; however, dreadful crimes may require dreadful punishments.

'I cannot make an order that you can never be released. However, I make it plain that I cannot envisage any circumstance which would justify the setting of a non-parole period. If I had the power to make an order that you were never to be released, I would unhesitatingly make that order.'

Justice had been done for all but the family of Suzanne Allen, who immediately called for the killers to again stand trial for her murder. They wanted closure, and the hung jury meant they were ineligible for victims' compensation.

Outside the court some family members spoke to the media, and it was a grief-stricken woman named Maureen Fox whose words were most telling. A foster carer, she had raised Gary O'Dwyer from when he was a baby.

'I have anger, contempt and hatred for two men who had no respect for another human being ... shame upon your souls.'

above: Workers gather at John Bunting's former home at 203 Waterloo
Corner Road to excavate the back yard. © *The Advertiser*, by Leon Mead

below: Detective Brian Swan emerges with a bag containing human bones.
© *The Advertiser*, by Mike Burton

Right: Detective Craig Patterson (centre, overalls) uses a sieve to locate human remains.

© *The Advertiser*, by Chris Mangan

Below: An aerial view of the excavation at 203 Waterloo Corner Road.

© *Newspix*, Mark Calleja

Top: Elizabeth Harvey, James Vlassakis's mother, in the Waterloo Corner Road house. The two victims buried in the back yard included Ray Davies, whom Harvey helped murder.

Harvey's eldest son Troy Youde (*above left*) and stepson David Johnson (*above right*), both victims of the killers.

Clinton Trezise (*right*) was Bunting's first victim, and came to his attention because of his association with Barry Lane (*below right*), the fifth victim. Thomas Trevilyan (*above*) helped Bunting and Wagner murder Lane, then became their next victim.

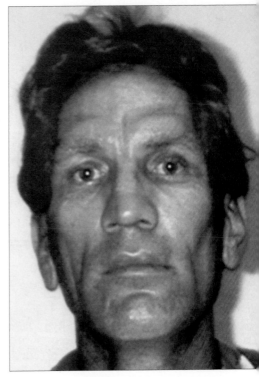

bove: Clinton Trezise's skeletal remains, found in Lower Light, SA.

© *Courtesy SA Police*

elow: Second and third victims Ray Davies and Suzanne Allen. They
et Bunting through Barry Lane.

Above: Mark Haydon with his wife, Elizabeth, who became the second last victim. Police attention after her disappearance slowed down the killers' pace.

Above: Fred Brooks, who was Elizabeth Haydon's nephew.

Right: Gary O'Dwyer, who resembled Troy Youde too much for Bunting's liking.

Above: Michael Gardiner's only crime
seemed to be annoying
Robert Wagner.

Left: Vlassakis's friend Gavin Porter,
the seventh victim.

Left: SA Deputy Director of Public Prosecutions Wendy Abraham QC at the opening on the Bunting and Wagner trial, October 2002.

Below: Police officers (L to R) Craig Patterson, Brian Swan and Bob Stapleton outside the SA Supreme Court building in September 2003.

TWENTY-FIVE

By August 2004 the Snowtown serial killings had faded in the memory of most South Australians, but not of those closest to the case. For police and prosecutors the job was not finished. For victims' families, still enduring the grief and horror inflicted upon them, justice was still one step away. It was time for the last of the suspected killers to stand trial.

Legal argument in the Mark Haydon trial began in May 2004, with the trial itself beginning three months later, on 2 August. Haydon had pleaded not guilty to the murders of Troy Youde, and his wife, Elizabeth. He had also pleaded not guilty to six counts of assisting offenders – helping Bunting, Wagner and Vlassakis hide the bodies of the six other victims found in barrels in the old Snowtown bank vault.

Again it was Wendy Abraham QC who would lead the prosecution case. It was her duty to show the jury how Haydon had played a role in two killings, and helped conceal six others – aiding and abetting the killers, allowing them to continue on their murderous venture. Her opening statement was skewed towards the role the prosecution alleged Haydon had played; it detailed every link between him and the worst case of serial killing in Australia's history.

'On 20 May 1999 the police discovered the disused bank at Snowtown, and stored in that bank six barrels containing eight bodies; the bodies of Michael Gardiner, Barry Lane, Gavin Porter, Troy Youde, Fred Brooks, Gary O'Dwyer, Elizabeth Haydon and David Johnson. Each of those victims had been murdered. At that time, the bank was being rented by John Bunting and the accused, Mark Haydon.

'After the bodies were stored in the vault, only four people actually entered the vault: John Bunting, Robert Wagner, James Vlassakis and the accused, Mark Haydon.

'Mark Haydon was seen in the bank, he was seen going in and out of the vault. His fingerprints were located in the bank, and his DNA located on items from within the bank. Eyewitness and forensic evidence ... links Mark Haydon, Bunting, Wagner and Vlassakis to the bank, to the vault and to the bodies.

'It is the Crown case that all four – Bunting, Wagner, Haydon and Vlassakis – had a role to play in either the commission of each of those murders, or in concealing the bodies of the victims. It's the Crown case that Bunting and Wagner committed each and every one of these murders, and that Vlassakis was involved with Bunting and Wagner in committing four of them. It is the Crown case that Mark Haydon was involved with them in committing the murders of two of those victims: Troy Youde, and his wife, Elizabeth Haydon; and that he assisted in concealing their bodies, and the bodies of six other victims; victims of Bunting, Wagner or Vlassakis.

'Ladies and gentlemen, it is alleged that Mark Haydon's involvement commenced with the murder of Troy Youde in August 1998. He was present and participated in that murder. The Crown says he committed that murder with Bunting, Wagner and Vlassakis. After his involvement in that murder, it is alleged Mark Haydon, together with Bunting, Wagner and Vlassakis, was actively involved in hiding the victims' bodies, concealing them to ensure the authorities did not become aware of the murders. This included Mark Haydon storing Troy Youde's body, and storing bodies of Bunting and Wagner's earlier victims Michael Gardiner, Barry Lane and Gavin Porter, and eventually, as time passed, their later victims Fred Brooks and Gary O'Dwyer.

'For a time Mark Haydon stored these bodies in the shed in the rear yard of his home. After his involvement in the murder of Troy Youde, and when he was already storing the bodies of other murder victims, it is alleged he was involved in the second murder with which he is charged, that is his own wife, Elizabeth Haydon. Again, it is alleged he committed this murder with Bunting and Wagner. Thereafter he was involved in storing her body, along with the others, initially in his shed, then in one of his vehicles, a Land Cruiser, and ultimately in the bank at Snowtown which he was jointly renting with John Bunting.

'After the bodies were stored in the bank, a further murder occurred: the murder of David Johnson. This murder was committed in the bank by Bunting, Wagner and Vlassakis, and the victim's body was stored in one of the barrels. Again Mark Haydon, a lessee of the bank, allowed the body to be stored there.

'That is why Mark Haydon is charged with two counts of murder – the murder of Troy Youde and the murder of Elizabeth Haydon – and six counts of assisting an offender, namely, assisting Bunting, Wagner or Vlassakis in storing, or permitting to be stored, the bodies of other of their victims: Michael Gardiner, Barry Lane, Gavin Porter, Fred Brooks, Gary O'Dwyer and David Johnson. The Crown says he concealed these bodies, and did so with the intention of assisting Bunting, Wagner or Vlassakis to avoid apprehension.

'That's the Crown case in a nutshell.'

Ms Abraham explained to the jury that a person is guilty of murder not only if they are responsible for the physical act itself, but also if they take part knowing what would, or could, occur.

She highlighted the fact Haydon and his legal team were not disputing that Bunting, Wagner and Vlassakis had committed the murders. Haydon, she said, would spend most of his time within this murderous circle, often listening to and joining in talk of paedophiles and what should be done to them.

'People he [Bunting] considered to be paedophiles were referred to as "rock spiders" and "dirties". He spoke of what he thought of paedophiles and what should be done to them. When Bunting spoke his demeanour was one of anger. He spoke in a very emphatic manner. When Robert Wagner was present he would reiterate what Bunting was saying. When Mark Haydon was present, although he was quieter, as he always was, he would nonetheless nod in agreement with what was being said ... on at least one of these occasions when Mark Haydon was present, John Bunting said, "We are vigilantes, we take care of paedophiles." The relevance of these conversations and, indeed, other conversations in which Mark Haydon was present, are twofold. One, the Crown says, in relation to conversations in which Mark Haydon was present, they reveal Mark Haydon's own attitude towards paedophiles. Secondly, and importantly, it is also evidence from which you may accept that Mark Haydon was aware of John Bunting's attitude towards paedophiles. Both of these aspects are relevant, particularly to the murder of Troy Youde, because it is the Crown case that a motive for the murder of Troy Youde is that he sexually abused James

Vlassakis. It follows that this is relevant then in proving Mark Haydon's involvement in the murder.'

Ms Abraham recounted the details of Troy Youde's murder in the home he had shared with Bunting and Vlassakis at Murray Bridge. It was the prosecution case that Haydon had been present during Youde's murder and had joined with Bunting, Wagner and Vlassakis in beating Youde with jack handles and wooden clubs before Youde was forced into the bathroom, tortured and murdered.

During Youde's murder, Bunting had listed the names of others he'd killed. The fact that he did this in the presence of Mark Haydon, it was alleged, suggested that Haydon knew about the previous killings. Even after the murder of Troy Youde, Ms Abraham told the jury, Haydon took part in the clean-up.

'Once Troy Youde was dead, John Bunting asked Vlassakis and Haydon to go to the shops and buy some more gloves and some heavy-duty garbage bags. At this stage Troy Youde's body was still in the bath. The two of them went to the shops in Mark Haydon's Land Cruiser and made the purchases and then returned to Burdekin Avenue. John Bunting and Robert Wagner were still there. Troy Youde's body, at this stage, was on the bathroom floor. Bunting told Wagner to make sure Troy Youde was dead and Wagner put his foot on Youde's chest, causing a noise to come out, and Bunting and Wagner laughed. Haydon and Vlassakis were present during this and watched. All four of them – Bunting, Wagner, Haydon and Vlassakis – put disposable gloves on because John Bunting said they had to be careful when handling dead bodies. Bunting put one garbage bag over Troy Youde's head, another over his middle and another over his feet and these were taped in place. As I said, Vlassakis and Haydon were present throughout, watching.

'All four – Bunting, Wagner, Haydon and Vlassakis – were involved in carrying Troy Youde's body out into the shed where the other bodies were already being stored. The four carried Troy Youde's body on a weights bar, two at the head and two at the feet. Initially they only went as far as the back door of the house when all four of them tried to put Troy Youde's body into a wardrobe which had the shelves kicked out, but Youde wouldn't fit and they didn't succeed in that. Again with the use of the weights bar, the body of Troy Youde was carried to the shed. It is the Crown case that there were already two barrels in the shed. In one were the bodies of Michael Gardiner and Barry Lane, and in the other the body of Gavin Porter. Troy Youde's body was left on the floor of the shed and the shed was locked. Vlassakis left the house briefly to get some methadone. At some stage after Vlassakis returned, whilst Bunting, Wagner and Haydon were still there, there was talk about what had happened. Bunting said that Youde had gone too quickly and that there wasn't enough pain, but he had said Youde had been made good. There were jokes between Bunting and Wagner. Bunting asked Vlassakis what it felt like as he had just committed murder. Mark Haydon, although present through this, didn't say anything.

'At some stage all four left the house to go to McDonald's and get something to eat, and then they returned to Burdekin Avenue. Before Mark Haydon and Robert Wagner left Murray Bridge to return to Adelaide, the house was cleaned up and Troy Youde's possessions were gathered up and put in garbage bags. Bunting and Vlassakis cleaned up the bathroom and Youde's bedroom, where there was some blood. Bunting and Wagner put some of Youde's property, his clothes, ID and paperwork into garbage bags. Bunting, Wagner and Haydon put those bags in the back of Mark Haydon's Land Cruiser and Mark Haydon and Robert Wagner drove off together in the Land Cruiser with Youde's property and the debris from the murder.

'Within a couple of days of Youde being murdered, John Bunting and Robert Wagner drove to Adelaide to buy a barrel. The barrel was purchased at Paramount Browns for $25. The barrel was taken and put in the shed at 3 Burdekin Avenue. The shed was kept locked and Bunting had the key.

'It is the Crown's case that Troy Youde's body in the barrel was moved to Mark Haydon's house at 4 Blackham Crescent, Smithfield Plains, and stored there for some time with other bodies until it was stored in Mark Haydon's Land Cruiser and ultimately in the Snowtown bank.

'The body of Troy Youde and the garbage bag which contained the debris cleaned up from the bathroom after Troy Youde's murder were found in the bank vault at Snowtown. In particular, in one of the garbage bags, with the property and bloodstained clothing of Troy Youde, were a number of disposable gloves. One of the gloves had a DNA typing on it consistent with that of Mark Haydon. Other gloves had DNA typings consistent with John Bunting and Robert Wagner. Property of Troy Youde's, of the type which the Crown says had been placed in Mark Haydon's Land Cruiser on the day of the murder, was found in Haydon's shed at 4 Blackham Crescent and in John Bunting's home at Bundarra Court, Craigmore.

'As I said, the body of Troy Youde was found in a barrel at the Snowtown bank. When his body was removed the gag was still in place with a sock in his mouth secured by adhesive tape. The rope was still around his neck. It is the Crown case that Mark Haydon is guilty of the murder of Troy Youde because he was a party to an understanding or agreement to murder Troy Youde, or at the very least a party to an assault in which he foresaw the possibility that Youde would be murdered, or he aided and abetted that murder. As a consequence, whilst all four played different roles, the law says it doesn't matter which role each played but each involved are equally responsible in the eyes of the law.'

Ms Abraham then detailed Haydon's role in moving and hiding bodies.

'The Crown alleges that shortly after the murder of Troy Youde, the three barrels containing the bodies of Barry Lane, Michael Gardiner, Gavin Porter and Troy Youde, the barrels that were stored in the shed at 3 Burdekin Avenue, Murray Bridge, had to be moved. Bunting was moving out ... there was no shed at the new premises and so somewhere else had to be found to store the bodies. This new storage place was the shed at Mark Haydon's home at 4 Blackham Crescent, Smithfield Plains. A truck was hired and Bunting and Wagner loaded up the barrels and they were taken away from Burdekin Avenue. Vlassakis next saw the barrels in the shed at Mark Haydon's home ... the obvious and logical inference is that he [Haydon] agreed for them to be stored there. From then on, John Bunting continued to have a place where, if he murdered someone, he could store the body.

'After Fred Brooks was murdered, it is alleged Bunting, Wagner and Vlassakis put Fred Brooks's body into garbage bags. His body was then carried out of the house [where Bunting was living in Murray Bridge] by Bunting and Wagner and put into the boot of a Torana which was parked in the rear yard. A couple of days after Fred Brooks's murder, Mark Haydon arrived in Murray Bridge driving his Land Cruiser, towing a car trailer. John Bunting and Mark Haydon put the Torana with, the Crown says, Fred Brooks's body still in the boot, onto the trailer and they drove the car away. Not long after that day, on the next occasion Vlassakis went to Blackham Crescent with John Bunting, he saw Mark Haydon working on the Torana. Bunting asked Haydon if Fred was happy, to which Haydon replied, "Yes". Bunting and Haydon went down the stairs into the pit of the shed, Vlassakis went a bit of the way down, and could see garbage bags on the floor. Bunting told him that it was Fred. Bunting asked Vlassakis about the smell – there was a smell apparent in the shed. It was this day that Vlassakis saw barrels in the shed.

'Within days of Mark Haydon taking the Torana from Murray Bridge, the Torana was registered in his name. The date of registration is 24 September 1998, and the vehicle was found at his home at Blackham Crescent at the time of his arrest.

'As with the murder of Troy Youde, the details necessary to access Fred Brooks's bank account were obtained from him by Bunting, Wagner and Vlassakis before he was murdered. Fred Brooks's Centrelink benefits were maintained, and his account accessed after his death. It is the Crown case that it is Mark Haydon who was given access to those benefits.'

The jury heard details, too, of how the body of the next murder victim, Gary O'Dwyer, was taken to Haydon's shed after the murder. O'Dwyer's lounge suite was also given to Haydon by Bunting, and was discovered by police when Haydon was arrested.

The next to die was Haydon's wife, Elizabeth. This was the second murder in which he was accused of actually taking part.

'Elizabeth Haydon was last seen alive on Saturday, November 21, 1998. At that time she was living at Blackham Crescent with Mark Haydon and her sister, [Gail Sinclair]. Elizabeth Haydon's children were away for the weekend staying with their uncle, Elizabeth Haydon's brother.

'Mark Haydon didn't actually do the physical act of killing. Indeed, the Crown says he wasn't even there at the time of the killing. It is the Crown case that Elizabeth Haydon was murdered pursuant to a plan made in advance by Bunting, Wagner and Haydon. Mark Haydon had a particular role in carrying out that plan. Elizabeth Haydon was to be murdered at Blackham Crescent, and for that to happen [Gail Sinclair] had to be taken away from the home. That was part of Mark Haydon's role in the murder of his wife. While Mark Haydon and [Gail Sinclair] were away from the house, John Bunting and Robert Wagner murdered Elizabeth Haydon and then, immediately upon Mark Haydon's return, all three – Mark Haydon, John Bunting and Robert Wagner – told stories to explain her whereabouts in an attempt to conceal her death, initially from [Gail Sinclair] and then from others, including police.

'During the trip home Mark Haydon stopped at a service station, telling [Gail Sinclair] he wanted to telephone home. When he came back to the car, he told [Gail Sinclair], 'We've got to get home, all hell has broken loose.'

'It is the Crown case that Elizabeth Haydon was dead by the time [Gail Sinclair] and Mark Haydon returned home ... [Gail Sinclair] was taken out of the house as part of a ruse, a set-up to make it look like she was doing her sister a favour. Mark Haydon was aware of the ruse and playing along with it.

'From the time of Sinclair's return, efforts were made by Mark Haydon, John Bunting and Robert Wagner to conceal Elizabeth Haydon's death … Mark Haydon pretended his wife was still alive, he didn't skip a beat, he told stories that matched up with Bunting and Wagner's.'

Ms Abraham guided the jury through the police questioning of Haydon about Elizabeth's disappearance. There were telltale discrepancies, the Crown alleged, in stories Haydon told his wife's family and friends. There was incriminating evidence found at his house.

The experienced prosecutor outlined evidence about the movement of the bodies in the barrels after Elizabeth Haydon's murder; the loading of Mark Haydon's four-wheel drive, which was towed first to the Joneses' property at Hoyleton, then their home in Snowtown. Finally Ms Abraham pointed to Haydon's role in leasing the old Snowtown bank, helping shift the bodies there and visiting regularly.

Most incriminating was the eyewitness evidence of James Vlassakis, detailing a visit to the bank where he and Haydon watched as Bunting and Wagner went inside the vault. The pair laughed about how quickly Elizabeth Haydon was 'festering away' – both Haydon and Vlassakis took a look.

'The Crown does not suggest that Haydon was involved in the mutilation of the bodies, or that he derived any particular enjoyment from being a participant or a witness to these activities. However, what the Crown says is important is that this visit demonstrates that Mark Haydon was a trusted person. He was part of these activities. He didn't extricate himself from the situation. He rendered assistance and he kept the group's activity secret. It also demonstrates that he had knowledge of what he was storing in the vault and that he was actively involved in the process.

'Mark Haydon's fingerprints were located on fixed items in the bank. For example, there were five separate fingerprints on the counter of the bank, and one on an internal doorframe. Mark Haydon's fingerprints were also detected on items locked away in the vault with the bodies, for example, his fingerprints were located on a plastic garbage bag with holes cut in it – the garbage bag had holes cut in it such that it might be worn by a person – and his fingerprints were on an empty hydrochloric acid container. A forensic pathologist who conducted the postmortem of the body of Elizabeth Haydon is of the view that her body did show some signs of having been immersed in acid, and one of the barrels that had liquid in it was weakly acidic.'

The jury heard that a number of garbage bags which contained debris collected after the murders of Fred Brooks and Troy Youde were located inside the vault. One bag contained Troy Youde's cut, bloodied T-shirt and knotted rope with his hair in the knot. Also inside were a number of disposable gloves with DNA typing consistent with the killers. Six gloves were matched to Robert Wagner, while one glove was found which had Bunting's DNA on one side and Troy Youde's on the other. One glove had DNA consistent with Mark Haydon's on it. In another garbage bag, also found in the vault, were more disposable gloves which were DNA matched to Bunting, Wagner and Haydon.

Forensic evidence, too, pointed to the storage of the bodies and barrels in Haydon's shed. During the police investigation into Elizabeth Haydon's disappearance, several police officers noted the smell of rotting flesh as they searched the shed. A forensic crime scene officer noticed an area of staining on the floor of a pit inside the shed. A test for traces of blood was positive and further tests detected traces of human DNA. Maggot casings were found in the pit, suggesting that a dead animal or human must have been nearby. Such casings were also found inside two garbage bags in the Snowtown bank. And a thorough search of the shed's pit and a car in the shed also located items in the name of Troy Youde, including a Medicare card and healthcare card, and mail addressed to Gavin Porter. A handcuff key, wire fashioned in the shape needed to pick the lock on the bank vault door, and disposable gloves were also found in the shed.

In Haydon's Land Cruiser police found another disposable glove with Bunting's fingerprint on it, and a letter in the name of Gavin Porter. In Haydon's station wagon were documents and items relating to Fred Brooks's banking and benefits, while Gary O'Dwyer's lounge suite was in Haydon's house.

'It is the Crown case that when you consider all the evidence relevant to each count, it will lead to the overwhelming and inescapable conclusion that Mark Haydon was involved in the murder of Troy Youde, that he was involved in the murder of Elizabeth Haydon, and that he was actively involved in concealing the bodies of six other victims, victims who had been murdered by Bunting, Wagner or Vlassakis, and he concealed those bodies for them with the intention of assisting them to escape apprehension.'

James Vlassakis and Elizabeth Haydon's sister – and Bunting's former fiancée – Gail Sinclair were both called as prosecution witnesses. Vlassakis recounted in great detail the role he said Haydon played in Troy Youde's murder. He also testified, as he had done in Bunting and Wagner's trial, about visits to Snowtown with Haydon and the others.

Sinclair spoke of the night her sister was murdered, and how Mark Haydon had taken her for a drive. When the pair returned, Elizabeth had vanished.

Sinclair described the close friendship between Haydon, Bunting and Wagner. 'They were like the three amigos,' she told the jury. 'They couldn't be separated. Wherever Bunting went, Mark went. To me, it appeared they were almost joined at the hip.'

The prosecution case relied heavily on Vlassakis's testimony, forensic evidence and victims' property found in Haydon's possession. There seemed little doubt that the barrels had been kept in the shed at Haydon's house, and that he'd leased the bank where they were found.

It was essential for Haydon's defence team to create doubt in the jurors' minds — provide alternative versions of events, explanations for some of their client's apparently suspicious actions. Marie Shaw QC and her team decided the best way to do this was with the assistance of Haydon himself. It was a gamble which opened the door to cross-examination, but on 10 November 2004, Mark Haydon took the stand in his own defence.

Mrs Shaw asked the questions — and wasted little time in getting to the point.

'Were you involved in the murder of your wife?'

'No.'

'Were you involved in the murder of Troy Youde?'

'No.'

'Prior to your arrest on 21 May 1999, did you have any inkling that there were human bodies in barrels at the bank at Snowtown?'

'No.'

'Had you ever heard of a person called Michael Gardiner before your arrest?'

'No.'

'Had you ever heard of a person called Gavin Porter before your arrest?'

'No.'

'Had you ever heard of a person called Gary O'Dwyer before your arrest?'

'No.'

'Did you see Troy Youde at any time in 1998?'

'No.'

Haydon's appearance on the stand presented an opportunity for him to be depicted as a typical 'battler' – a forty-six year old who had spent the past five and a half years in jail, having been unwittingly caught up in Australia's worst ever case of serial killing. The jury was shown glimpses of Haydon's personal life, such as his brother's death in a car accident at age twenty-six, and the fact that he had left school without completing Year 11.

Haydon's first job was at the General Motors Holden plant in Adelaide's north, after which he was in and out of work. It was at a welding course in 1989 that he met John Bunting. He met Elizabeth Haydon in 1994, formed a relationship and she moved in with him. Elizabeth was interested in ceramics, and she and Mark undertook courses with a view to setting up their own business. The business was being discussed with Bunting's de facto, Elizabeth Harvey, who was also interested in ceramics.

In 1996 there was a dispute between the Haydons and Elizabeth Harvey which drove a wedge between Bunting and Mark Haydon. Their friendship resumed in 1998 when Bunting showed up out of the blue. That same year Haydon bought the house at 4 Blackham Crescent, Smithfield Plains, where he lived with Elizabeth, who was by then his wife. Also living there were two of Elizabeth's sons, and her sister, Gail Sinclair, who began a relationship with Bunting.

Throughout his testimony Haydon referred to his once-friends as 'Bunting', 'Wagner' and 'Vlassakis', perhaps hoping to distance himself from his former mates.

After her client was settled on the stand, Mrs Shaw's questions turned to Elizabeth Haydon. Mark Haydon claimed to have still loved her. They were trying for a baby – he certainly didn't want her dead.

'We know this from the medical records that your wife was having pregnancy tests in late 1998?'

'Yes.'

'Were your taking her to the doctor?'

'Yes.'

'Were you and your wife endeavouring to have a child at this time?'

'Yes.'

'Was that the position right up until the time your wife disappeared?'

'Yes.'

'You have heard that your wife suffered from genital herpes?'

'Yes.'

'Did that concern you in relation to your efforts to have a child?'

'No, because it wasn't contagious unless it was flaring up.'

'In your relationship you were able to manage that so it wasn't an issue?'

'Yes.'

Haydon's attention was then turned to the other murder with which he was charged.

'Can I take you to Murray Bridge ... did you and your wife ever visit Murray Bridge after you saw Mr Bunting again in 1998?'

'Yes, we dropped him off there a couple of times and also picked him up a couple of times.'

'Did you go into the house at any stage with your wife?'

'No, we only ever dropped him off or picked him up at the end of his street.'

'You know of the charges against you? That you were at Burdekin Avenue when Mr Youde was killed in August 1998; that's the allegation against you.'

'Yes, I'm aware of that allegation.'

'Did you ever go into the premises at Burdekin Avenue in 1998 at any time when Troy Youde was there?'

'No.'

'Had you met Troy Youde before 1998?'

'Yes.'

'When?'

'In 1994.'

'Had you seen him since 1994?'

'Yes.'

'When?'

'Several times between '94 at Kilsby Street, it was where his mother was living, a few times at Tilshead Street where Marcus Johnson was living.'

'Is that when he was living with Marcus Johnson?'

'Yes. I think once up at a place called Bakara in the Riverland and that was it.'

Still one of the most damaging areas of evidence had to be tackled. Under oath, Haydon admitted he had stored the barrels in his garage, and then helped move them to Snowtown. He admitted leasing the bank with Bunting and shifting the barrels there. His explanation was that he had not known the barrels contained human remains, that Bunting first told him the barrels contained animal skins and later that there were actually kangaroo carcasses inside. Haydon told the court he never looked in the barrels and had no sense of smell, so never had reason to doubt Bunting's story. Bunting had first asked Haydon to take the barrels when he was moving house.

'On that topic, did Mr Bunting speak to you about that?'

'Yes, he said he had no shed at the place where he was moving to and he needed somewhere to store what he had in the shed.'

'Did you agree?'

'Yes.'

'Did some property arrive at Blackham after that conversation?'

'After that conversation, yes.'

'Before the property arrived, did you know exactly what it was going to be?'

'No, I didn't.'

'What did Mr Bunting bring to Blackham?'

'One morning him and Wagner came around in a truck, had some drums on it, some garbage bags.'

'What did they do with them?'

'Drums went into the corner of the garage and the garbage bags on the floor in front of the drums.'

'How many drums did you see?'

'I remember about four.'

'The garbage bags, did they stay on the shed floor or were they placed somewhere else?'

'No, I moved them down into the cellar out of the way.'

The Judge then asked, 'Is the cellar what has been referred to by some of the witnesses as the "pit"?'

'Yes.'

Haydon also explained that when he had moved a car from Bunting's house at Murray Bridge to his own home, he had been unaware that the body of Fred Brooks was in the boot.

'How did you come to do that?'

'Bunting was at my place with the truck in the morning.'

'Yes.'

'And he asked me if I still wanted the Torana back.'

'What did you say?'

'I said "Yes, I do".'

'Did you go and get it?'

'Yes, later that afternoon.'

'Did you open up the boot?'

'No, when I first had a look at the car at Murray Bridge I tried to open the boot and the key I had wouldn't fit.'

'So what did you do? Did you try once you got it down to Blackham?'

'Yes.'

'What did you do about that?'

'I had some old Holden keys, I just kept trying keys in the lock to see if I could get it open.'

'Did you get it open?'

'Yes I did.'

'When you got it open, did you see anything in there?'

'Spare tyre ... a few scraps of paper.'

'We have heard that luminal testing of that boot [for blood] was negative. Did you see anything in there that looked as though it might have had any garbage bag in there?'

'No.'

★   ★   ★

Next Haydon gave the jury his version of events surrounding his wife's disappearance. The night before, he said, her two sons had gone to stay at their uncle Garion's house. During the day, Haydon said he worked around the house while Elizabeth and her sister went to a doll-making class. Bunting was there, as he often was, and Robert Wagner came to visit.

That night, Haydon took Gail Sinclair for a drive.

'You did take [Gail Sinclair] to Reynella?'

'Yes.'

'How did that come about?'

'Elizabeth asked me to go.'

'Which car did you go in?'

'Bunting's Marquis.'

'Is there any reason why you didn't go in your car?'

'Mine had very little fuel and I didn't have a lot of money at the time.'

'How was it, what did Elizabeth say to you to persuade you to take [Gail Sinclair] to Reynella?'

'She said [Gail] wanted to go and have a look at a dog to mate with her two females, that she didn't know where Reynella was and John Bunting had to be somewhere at some point that evening, he said he did.'

'Did you say anything about your car and petrol when Elizabeth asked you that?'

'I said, "Well, I haven't got the fuel or the money to get that".'

'How was that problem solved?'

'Bunting offered to let me use his car and gave me $20 for gas.'

Haydon said he and Gail Sinclair set off about five o'clock, reached the meeting place at Reynella in Adelaide's south, and waited. The dog owners failed to arrive, so they began driving home. On the way Haydon stopped to make a telephone call.

'Where did you stop to do that?'

'I tried to make a phone call outside the Bolivar Caravan Park.'

'When you say you tried, you stopped at the phone box?'

'Yes.'

'What was your reason for trying or wanting to make a phone call?'

'I just thought I would check to see if she [Elizabeth] wanted like milk or bread or anything like that when I was on my way home.'

'What happened when you first tried?'

'The phone seemed to ring out, but I wasn't sure whether it was — it had actually rung out and she didn't answer or if the phone booth I was using was out of order.'

'Did you stop again?'

'Yes.'

'Where did you stop?'

'Salisbury.'

On the second attempt, Haydon said Bunting answered the phone.

'He just said, "All hell has broken out. Your wife has gone into the bedroom ranting and locked herself in there." I asked him what was the problem and he said it would be better if he explained when I got home.'

'Did you return home?'

'Yes.'

'When you got home, who was there?'

'Bunting and Wagner, my wife was in the bedroom still.'

'Did [Gail Sinclair] come inside with you?'

'Yes.'

'Can you tell us what was said?'

'Bunting told me that my wife had made a sexual advance towards him, he rejected her and she stormed into the bedroom.'

'Did he and [Gail Sinclair] stay there or go somewhere else?'

'No, they went into the kitchen.'

'Did he tell you what the nature of the advance was?'

'Not at that stage.'

'Did he say what his response was to the advance?'

'He said he refused it.'

'What did you do?'

'I went down to the bedroom to talk to my wife.'

'What happened when you went to the bedroom?'

'I knocked on the door, went in, asked for her side of the story.'

'What was your wife doing when you went into the bedroom?'

'Lying on the bed.'

'Did she appear happy or unhappy?'

'She appeared like she had been crying.'

'You told us what you said, did she respond to that?'

'She accused me of sleeping with [Gail Sinclair].'

'What were her words?'

'I can't remember her exact words but she said, "You've been sleeping with Gail", and she also called me a lazy good-for-nothing.'

Haydon said his wife would not accept his denials. He left the room, telling her he would return when she was prepared to 'start talking sense'. Bunting and Gail Sinclair went and got some dinner while Haydon stayed at the house with Wagner. Within moments Elizabeth came 'storming' out of the bedroom yelling that her 'boyfriend' was coming to pick her up. She 'staggered' in drunk at four o'clock the next morning and passed out on their bed.

According to Haydon's version of events, Wagner had gone home but John Bunting had stayed the night with Gail Sinclair. The following morning Bunting and Sinclair went out.

'Did you leave the house?'

'Yes.'

'Before you left the house did you speak to your wife?'

'Yes.'

'What was said?'

'I asked – again asked her where she had been, who she had been with, she said it was nobody I knew. She didn't intimate whether it was male or female. She said she was going to get up and have a shower and go again. I asked her to stay put at least until I got back from seeing my father. She said she would. I also asked her just to think about what she is doing and what she really wants to do.'

That night, Haydon said, his wife never came home. He went to pick up the boys from her brother.

'When you got to Garion's place, did you say something to Garion about Elizabeth?'

'Yes, after he asked a few questions.'

'What did you tell him about where Elizabeth was?'

'I told him that she was at home sleeping.'

'Why did you tell him that?'

'Because the boys were within earshot at the time and I didn't want to be upsetting them.'

The next day, Monday 23 November, Haydon sent the boys to school but they didn't return home. When he went to his mother-in-law's to look for them, he told her Elizabeth had taken off. Haydon found the boys back at

Garion Sinclair's house. They had told him their mum was missing.

'Did you speak to Garion about what was going to happen to the boys?'

'Yes.'

'What was said about that?'

'... as far as the boys were concerned, he said they would be better off with him and I agreed, I said, "If they wish to stay here they are quite" – I was quite happy for them to.'

'Did you say anything about speaking to them?'

'Yes, I said, "I'll ask them"; make sure they definitely wanted to stay there.'

'Was something said about the welfare?'

'Yes, he also said that he had been to welfare that day and they advised him to report my wife missing to the police, if the welfare needed to serve papers on her.'

'Did you say anything about the topic of reporting her missing?'

'He asked me if I was going to and I said, well, it would be a waste of time me reporting her missing if he was going to do it.'

Haydon told the court that during later visits to Garion Sinclair he had told his brother-in-law that Elizabeth had run off, and that he'd lied at first so the boys were not upset.

On Monday, 30 November 1998, the police visited Haydon's house. He was out at a training course, but Gail Sinclair was home. This was the day, Haydon admitted, that he helped move the barrels from his garage.

'When you came home from the course, was something said by [Gail Sinclair] on the topic of the police?'

'Yes, she informed me that the police had been there

looking around, they wanted to have a look in the garage, which was locked that particular day.'

'Did you go anywhere?'

'I went down to Wagner's place.'

'Did you have Bunting's phone number?'

'At the time I was unsure as to whether it was in the house anywhere.'

'Why did you go to Wagner's place?'

'Because I knew he had Bunting's phone number.'

'Why did you want to contact Bunting?'

'Because I wanted him to get – to remove what I assumed to be stolen property he had stored in my garage.'

'Had you seen items in your garage that you thought were stolen property?'

'Yes, a couple of stereos, fire extinguisher, electrical water pump.'

'You told us Mr Wagner placed some drums in your shed.'

'Yes.'

'Did he tell you at the time what was in the drums?'

'He said it was animal skins that he was tanning.'

'After you had been to Mr Wagner's place, did you go back to Blackham Crescent?'

'Yes, we all did.'

'When you got back there what happened, what did you do?'

'[Gail Sinclair] was asked to go in the family room to keep an eye out for the police. Wagner had a look up in the ceiling.'

'Was something said about that before he did that?'

'Yes, we had the idea to see if there was any room – just to see if we could put the property up there. Then, after Wagner came down, I just said, "There's no point in putting it up there because if the police are looking around they are going to look up there eventually anyway.'"

'Once you said that, what happened?'

'Then we went out to the garage and just had a look at everything. Bunting asked what I wanted done with the four-wheel drive because I told him earlier that I was worried about having too many vehicles in the front yard.'

'You said that the registration of the four-wheel drive had expired back at the end of September. Where had the four-wheel drive been located since September; that is from the end of September to the end of November?'

'Parked in front of my bedroom window parallel to the house facing north.'

'What was said? You were about to tell us what was said about the four-wheel drive on this occasion after Mr Wagner had a look in the ceiling.'

'Yes.'

'What happened then?'

'Well, Bunting suggested he take everything he put in my shed that night, it wouldn't all fit in his vehicle so he decided to take my four-wheel drive, store that for me and use that to transport what he had in the garage.'

'That was unregistered at the time?'

'Yes.'

'What was done about transporting it?'

'Him and Wagner went out and hired a trailer.'

'What happened to the four-wheel drive in relation to the trailer?'

'It was reversed into under the carport, the drums, the garbage bags, more electrical items that he had stored in there, loaded into the four-wheel drive and then it was driven onto the trailer.'

'Then was there any conversation on the topic of where this was all going?'

'He just told me that a friend of his out in the country would store it for him and if I wanted – when I wanted to actually start working on the vehicle I could just let him know and just go up and pick it up.'

'Did you help with the garbage bags?'

'Yes.'

'Was there a problem when you were helping with the garbage bags?'

'Yes, when I got one up out of the cellar walking towards the four-wheel drive ... the bottom fell out of the bag.'

'What did you then do?'

'I then just looked to see what was fallen out of the bag, it was sort of clothing, several used gloves, some other general rubbish, a little bit of paperwork. Would have been soiled clothing, gloves, I didn't know what was on it. I had whatever it was on my hands so I grabbed a pair of gloves.'

'Did you have the gloves in your garage?'

'Yes.'

'For what purpose did you have the gloves there?'

'Cleaning up around the place, picking up old slimy dog bones off the lawn before I mowed it.'

'Did you know that there was a box of gloves located in a wardrobe in your bedroom?'

'Yes, because when my wife and I did the first aid course they advised us it would be a very good idea to carry one pair of gloves in your pocket or purse.'

'Did you collect the material that had fallen out of the bag?'

'Yes, Bunting and Wagner helped.'

'What did you do with it?'

'Put it into a fresh garbage bag.'

'What did you do with the gloves that you wore?'

'From memory, threw them into the bag as well.'

The garbage bag incident was Haydon's explanation for how his DNA came to be among the contents, mixed with debris from Troy Youde's murder.

Next he had to explain his visits to Hoyleton and Snowtown.

'Can I then come to 1999, in particular, at some stage did you meet or see Kathy and Simon Jones?'

'Yes.'

'When was it you first saw them, or in what circumstances did you first see them in 1999?'

'[Gail Sinclair] had just been admitted to hospital. I didn't really want to sit in the house on my own all night and Bunting said he was going up to see Simon and Kathy, asked me if I wanted to come along for the drive.'

'Which vehicle did you go in?'

'A Volvo that Bunting had purchased.'

'Did something happen to that Volvo?'

'Yes, the engine blew up at Lochiel.'

'What did you do then?'

'Walked the 30 kilometres to Snowtown.'

'What happened when you got there?'

'We went to the Joneses' house.'

'Did you go to the Joneses' house at Hoyleton at some stage?'

'After that, yes.'

'So when you went to Snowtown, how did that fit in with going to their house at Hoyleton?'

'They were still moving property down from Hoyleton to Snowtown.'

'When you got to the Joneses' house, what did you do?'

'Knocked on the door, it was early hours of the morning so it took a little while for them to answer. Kathy invited us in and we stayed the night.'

'Did you return to Adelaide?'

'The following day, yes.'

'How did you get back there?'

'Simon drove us back.'

'Did you have a shower while you were at the Joneses' on that occasion?'

'Yes, I did that morning.'

'You said there was a shift from Hoyleton to Snowtown. Did you help with that shift on one day or more than one day?'

'From memory about two or three days.'

'What was shifted on the day or days that you helped?'

'Some vehicles, a couple of vehicles, just general household stuff he had in the shed at Hoyleton.'

'When you went to Hoyleton, did you see the Land Cruiser?'

'Yes.'

'Did you say anything to Bunting about that?'

'I don't remember actually saying anything to him about it.'

'Did you see drums in the back of the Land Cruiser?'

'The vehicle still appeared the same as when it left my place.'

'Was the vehicle or the Land Cruiser taken to Snowtown?'

'Yes.'

'How did it get there?'

'It was taken down there on a trailer.'

'Who organised the trailer?'

'Bunting, from memory.'

'On that occasion, when you helped moving the Land Cruiser to Snowtown on the trailer, can you say whether or not you had a shower on that occasion?'

'I think I did.'

'Can I come to the lease [bank lease]: when did you first hear anything about the possibility of a lease of a bank at Snowtown? First of all, what month?'

'January.'

'Who raised it with you?'

'Kathy Jones, she was actually talking to Bunting.'

'What did you hear said?'

'She just said, "The bank across the road is up for rent."'

'Did you hear the circumstances in which it was raised with Bunting as to why he might have an interest in such a place?'

'He had . . . just said he wanted to get away for a while.'

'Were you there when the lease was obviously signed?'

'Yes, I was.'

'How did you come to be a signatory to the lease?'

'Bunting and I were toying with the idea of going into business together and we were going to – my understanding was we were going to use it for storage of equipment and finished product and when Bunting was filling out the lease he started writing my Christian name and I asked him why he was writing my name on there.'

'What did he tell you?'

'He said, "If you're going to be part of the business, you may as well go on the lease." I then told him, "Use my former name because I don't want it to get back to Centrelink."'

'Your former name is Mark Lawrence?'

'Yes.'

'Did you sign the lease?'

'Yes.'

'Were you present looking at the bank before that day in the presence of the Michaels?'

'Yes.'

'Was anything said by Bunting about what he would store in the bank?'

'He told Mrs Michael that he would be storing the equipment, some finished product, and he asked her if he could store some drums of chemicals.'

'Was there any conversation about a key to the vault?'

'Yes, Bunting asked her if there was a key to the vault.'

'What was said about that?'

'Mrs Michael said, "Yes" there was one, she would drop it in.'

Haydon admitted helping move the barrels into the vault. He admitted to travelling to Snowtown at Bunting's request to pay the bank rent. However there was another, more sinister visit he needed to address before the jury.

Earlier in the trial, Vlassakis had told of a visit involving himself, Haydon, Bunting and Wagner. They had taken cement which was to be poured into the barrels so they could be dumped at sea. Vlassakis claimed he and Haydon had gone into the vault, then left as Bunting and Wagner began to cut up victims' bodies.'

Now, as he sat in the witness box, Mark Haydon told a very different story about that journey to Snowtown.

'Did you take anything with you in the car?'

'Yes.'

'What was placed in your car?'

'Buckets and hoses, some white shopping bags, this is at Bundarra [Bunting's house]. Then we went to Mofflin Road [Wagner's house], John told me to reverse my car up to the back of Wagner's car. Then transferred some bags of concrete from Wagner's car into mine, then some more shopping bags were put in the car. Then we went up to Snowtown.'

'Was there anything said about the reason for going to Snowtown that day?'

'He [Bunting] said he was going to cut the roos up to reduce the space that they were taking up and then eventually fill the drums with acid and get rid of them – and concrete.'

'When you got there, did you take anything into the bank?'

'I helped move the concrete in and I handed him – handed Bunting some bottles of acid that were in the back of my vehicle.'

'When was the acid placed in the vehicle?'

'Earlier that day.'

'Where at?'

'A hardware store in Salisbury.'

'Do you remember how many bottles there were?'

'From memory, three or four.'

'Did you have any intention of being involved in the cutting up of the roo carcasses?'

'None.'

'Was there a reason for that?'

'I think the sight of rotting animal carcasses tends to make me vomit.'

'Did you take a change of clothes?'

'No.'

'How long did you stay at the bank on that occasion?'

'One, possibly two hours.'

'What were you doing at the time?'

'I was just wandering around in the foyer, looking at the Joneses' electrical gear.'

'Did you put any gloves on at any time when you were in the bank?'

'No.'

'At any time when you went to Snowtown did you ever put on any gloves?'

'No.'

'Did you see, first of all, Mr Bunting in any different clothes at any time during this period that you were at the bank?'

'Yes, he put on a pair of white disposable overalls over the top of what he was wearing.'

'What about Mr Wagner, did you see him wear something different?'

'His CFS [Country Fire Service] overalls.'

'What about Mr Vlassakis, did you see him wearing anything different?'

'Not from memory, no.'

'At any time when you were there, did you see anybody come out of the vault wearing gloves?'

'No.'

'After this one or two hours, where did you go?'

'Then went over to the Joneses'.'

'What happened there?'

'Bunting, Wagner and Vlassakis all had showers.'

'Did you have a shower?'

'No.'

'Then where did you go?'

'Back to Adelaide, as far as I can remember.'

'When you were at the bank and Bunting and Wagner and Vlassakis were there and you told us that you were looking at electrical equipment when Bunting and Wagner had changed their clothes – referring to that time when you were told they were cutting up roos' carcasses — did you ever yourself go into the vault on that occasion?'

'No.'

'Did you ever put your head through the plastic to see what they were doing?'

'No.'

'Did you ever make any comment on the topic of your stomach?'

'Yes.'

'What did you say?'

'From memory, I said to Jamie, "I don't know how you can stand doing that because I wouldn't be able to stomach it."'

During his two days of testimony, Haydon explained away other aspects of the case against him. He denied knowledge of victims' property found in his cars or house, except for Gary O'Dwyer's lounge suite, which he said Bunting had given him. He acknowledged taking Jamie Vlassakis to visit a doctor, but hadn't known Vlassakis was impersonating a murder victim at the time. He denied any knowledge that the bank accounts of Fred Brooks or Gavin Porter were being accessed.

After two days of explanations and denials, Haydon had to face cross-examination. Wendy Abraham probed his accounts of various events, often flustering Haydon to the extent that he would pause for long periods of time before answering her questions. In particular, Ms Abraham queried Haydon on the visit to the vault when the bodies were mutilated.

'Why didn't you say, "Hang on, if this is what we are doing, I don't want to be involved in this?"'

'I thought he meant loading and unloading of vehicles.'

'When you were sitting in the car did you tell him, "I don't want to be involved in this"?'

'Well, I had previously told him that I wouldn't be going in there to the vault if they were doing anything with the roos' carcasses.'

'Why did you think the help was sought for loading and unloading?'

'Concrete, bags of concrete, I assumed wouldn't be very light.'

'But there was already Mr Wagner, he was quite a tall chap wasn't he, or is he?'

'Yes.'

'Mr Vlassakis was already there?'

'Yes.'

'And Mr Bunting?'

'Yes.'

'Didn't need four people to carry a few bags of concrete, did it?'

Haydon was feeling the pressure as Ms Abraham probed his version of events.

'You have told us there was acid that day, where did that come from?'

'That had been purchased earlier.'

'By you?'

'Not by me, but in my presence.'

'When earlier?'

'Mid afternoon.'

'Before you were asked to go for a drive?'

'Yes.'

'When it was purchased – that is, the acid – you were in your car?'

'Yes.'

'Put in the back, was it?'

'Yes.'

'Still, when you were asked a little later to drive to Snowtown and give him a hand if needed, you didn't think at that stage it had to do with acid?'

'I'd actually forgotten about the acid at that point.'

'Anyway, you get to the bank and the property is unloaded?'

'Yes.'

'The vault is opened?'

'Yes.'

'All four of you went in?'

'No, I didn't.'

'You stayed out?'

'Yes.'

'Did Mr Bunting say, "Look, Mr Haydon, you'd better stay out"?'

'There was no need to because I would have.'

'You could have walked in any time you wanted?'

'I could have.'

'There was talk going on inside the vault?'

'I couldn't make out what was actually being said.'

'Could you hear voices?'

'I could hear voices, yes.'

'Bit of laughter?'

'On the odd occasion.'

'And you just stood outside the vault?'

'I was looking at the Joneses' electrical gear.'

'For possibly up to a couple of hours?'

'Yes, possibly.'

'Didn't once put your head in and say, "Hang on, how long are we going to be?"'

'I didn't put my head in, but I stood next to the opening and asked them.'

'The opening had a split in it?'

'Yes.'

'You just stood there and didn't move the split at all?'

'Just slightly, but I never looked in.'

'Moved the split, looked the other way, and asked, "How long are you going to be?"'

'Yes.'

'Mr Haydon, that day you were in the vault when the barrels were opened, I suggest. You say that just didn't happen?'

'Didn't happen.'

'And there was talk about Troy, just didn't happen?'

'Not that I heard.'

'I suggest you were in the vault when there was talking about Troy – didn't happen?'

'Didn't happen.'

'The barrel was opened and your wife was in it and there was talk about your wife, just didn't happen?'

'Didn't happen.'

Ms Abraham also attempted to cast doubt over Haydon's claims that he had leased the Snowtown bank with Bunting for a business venture they were embarking on.

'From that day, what did you do in relation to the business?'

'Asked Bunting when it was going to start producing.'

'Apart from asking Bunting when it was going to start producing, what did you actually do in relation to the business?'

'Nothing, actually.'

There were questions too about why he'd allowed the barrels to be moved into his newly leased 'business' premises.

'By that stage you were a joint lessee for this bank?'

'Yes.'

'You believed it was going to be for the business?'

'Yes.'

'Did it occur to you to ask, "What have the barrels got to do with the business that we are going to set up?"'

'No.'

In the final moments of her cross-examination, Ms Abraham tested Haydon's nerve. The atmosphere in the courtroom was electric, and each and every juror was watching Haydon intently.

'The situation is, isn't it, that you were involved with John Bunting, Robert Wagner and James Vlassakis in murdering Troy Youde?'

'No.'

'That you had been told before that John Bunting and Robert Wagner had killed people?'

'No.'

'That after the murder of Troy Youde, a barrel with his body, and two other barrels, with Gavin Porter, Barry Lane and Michael Gardiner, were brought to your premises, and you knowingly stored those barrels, that is, knowing that there were bodies in there?'

'No.'

'Just didn't happen?'

'I didn't know what the barrels really had in them, no.'

'I suggest after that time Fred Brooks's body was stored in your shed.'

'No, not to my knowledge.'

'Gary O'Dwyer's?'

'Not to my knowledge.'

'And you were involved with the murder of your wife?'

'No.'

'None of that happened?'

'No.'

'And you've got no idea what was in the barrels in a vault that you were renting?'

'No, I didn't know what was in them.'

'Never asked?'

'No.'

'And you were renting the bank at Snowtown with John Bunting, I suggest, to store the bodies of victims of the murders that you were involved in and the victims of murders that John Bunting, Robert Wagner and Vlassakis had been involved in?'

'No.'

'Just didn't happen?'

'No.'

In her summing up of the defence case, Marie Shaw described Mark Haydon as a man who loved his wife and believed he was loved in return. He was not involved in her murder.

'Mr Haydon did not join with Bunting, Wagner and Vlassakis in these atrocities. The prosecution, at the very least, has not proved beyond reasonable doubt that he joined with them. At the very least you must be left with doubt about the proof of each of the charges. The prosecution has not proved beyond a reasonable doubt that Vlassakis is a credible, trustworthy witness. You must be left with a doubt about the proof of each of the counts.

'Mr Lyons, Mr Abbott and myself have endeavoured to assist Mr Haydon to present his answer to the charges to the court. Our responsibility for him has now come to an end. We now pass him into your hands and we ask you find him not guilty on each of the counts.'

Ms Abraham urged the jury to convict.

'I suggest the Crown has proved that Mark Haydon

became involved in these activities with the murder of Troy Youde. He was party to that murder, in particular circumstances, and thereafter he stored the body, not only of Troy Youde, but the bodies of Bunting and Wagner's previous victims and thereafter he continued to agree to store the bodies of victims killed by Bunting or Wagner, and in some instances Vlassakis. He did so knowingly, and he did so obviously with the intention of assisting them to escape apprehension – as I said they were pretty successful for an extraordinarily long period of time.

'He then became involved in the murder of his wife. He stored her body, as he stored the others. He continued to associate and indeed was much closer in association. He was involved in the activities in the bank. He was involved in activities relating to the barrels. And then, when the next victim was murdered – indeed, there's quite a long gap you might think, because of the fact the police had been involved looking for Elizabeth Haydon – then, in May 1999, whilst you might think he's getting the benefits from the victims, two of the victims whose bodies he's storing, he knows or believes that David Johnson has also been murdered, and he continues the lease allowing that body to be stored with the others in the bank.

'I suggest that we've proved the case in relation to the murder of Troy Youde, Elizabeth Haydon, and, indeed, that he was assisting them escape apprehension in relation to the other six bodies. That is a matter now for you.'

On Wednesday, 15 December 2004, the jury in Mark Haydon's trial retired to consider its verdicts. The legal teams, police and media virtually camped outside the courtroom door as South Australia again held its collective breath, waiting to see if yet another man would be convicted over the infamous crimes which had scarred the state forever.

Three days later the jury returned briefly, to tell Justice Sulan they were decided on five of the assisting offenders charges, but still deadlocked on the sixth, and undecided on the two murder charges. They were sent back for further deliberations.

The following afternoon, Sunday, 19 December, the jury returned to say nothing had changed – and nothing would.

Mark Haydon was convicted of five counts of assisting John Bunting, Robert Wagner and James Vlassakis. The jury had decided Haydon helped hide and move the barrels, knowing there were human bodies inside.

However, the jury was deadlocked on the question of whether Haydon took part in the murders of Troy Youde and Haydon's wife, Elizabeth, and was also unable to agree on the sixth and final count of assisting in relation to the murder of David Johnson.

It was a victory of sorts for Mark Haydon and his legal team; by law, he was not a killer. However, he was now a criminal, convicted of helping to cover up five murders, assisting serial killers as they continued their evil acts. Haydon could have prevented victims' deaths. Instead, he concealed them.

As Justice Sulan remanded Haydon in custody, to be sentenced later, the prosecution indicated that they would again force him to stand trial for murder. Much had changed in the nine months after the Haydon verdict. South Australia had a new Director of Public Prosecutions and deputy Wendy Abraham QC, who had prosecuted all of the Snowtown accused, had resigned. It was no secret the public prosecutor's office was under-funded, under-staffed and morale was low.

Behind the scenes, a deal had been brokered between prosecutors and Haydon's defence team, which would see the now 46-year-old walk free far sooner than anyone had expected.

On Friday 16 September, in a surprise court hearing, the two remaining murder charges against Haydon – over the deaths of his wife and Troy Youde - were dropped. The trade-off was that he pleaded guilty to assisting Bunting, Wagner and Vlassakis in the cover-up that followed those killings.

The deal saved the taxpayer the expense of another lengthy court battle, and marked the end of the Snowtown murder trials. All that was left was for Haydon to be sentenced for the seven counts of assisting offenders for which he had now been convicted. Having already spent seven years behind bars, it seemed certain he would serve only a few more. If that.

The justice system had found Haydon was not a killer. He had, however, helped conceal the horrific crimes of his serial killer friends, even to the point of hiding victims' bodies in his own garage.

Mark Ray Haydon may soon be free, but will forever have blood on his hands.

TWENTY-SIX

It is a routine which will change little for the rest of John Bunting's life. Every morning, at about 7.30 a.m., the breakfast trolley rattles its way from one prison cell to another, eventually stopping at Bunting's door. The small hatch in the door is opened and Bunting is allowed to choose from two types of breakfast cereal. His choice is scooped into a plastic bowl, and he's handed half a litre of milk – his ration for the day. Four slices of toast complete his morning meal.

Once breakfast is over, Bunting must stand against the back wall of his cell as the door is unlocked and then step outside while it is searched by prison officers. Finally he is handed a mop to complete his morning 'muck out'.

At the time of writing, John Bunting is being held in E Division in Yatala Prison, South Australia's maximum security jail, located in Adelaide's northern suburbs. His cell has a small television, a kettle and some personal effects like a toothbrush and razor. The room has concrete walls and floor, a single window, and a stainless steel toilet and basin. There are two bunk beds, but Bunting has no cellmate. He brags to other prisoners how he's told authorities he'll attack anyone placed in his cell, so he's left alone. At least for now.

After Bunting has completed his morning routine, he is allowed into the Association Area, a room where inmates gather to watch television, play games and drink coffee. Later he is free to move into the weightlifting area or exercise yard. While Bunting does not lift weights and plays no sport, he often walks around, stopping to talk with other inmates.

John Bunting has learned quickly how to survive in prison. Although a short man, he is strongly built and has struck fear into fellow inmates with his bravado and talk of violence. He makes much of his reputation as Australia's worst serial killer. Bunting has attacked another inmate who belittled him on at least one occasion, and he has been known to arm himself with a pencil which he regularly dips in faeces, warning others that the stab wound from the pencil would not be nearly as bad as the infection they would get afterwards.

Those who choose to listen say Bunting speaks incessantly of escaping from prison and taking revenge on those who put him there. He mentions police officers by name and describes what he would like to do to them. Bunting also brags about his crimes, about the pain he inflicted on his victims as they were tortured. John Bunting's new life is one of fantasy, spent reliving all he has done, and yearning for the chance to do it again.

Only every now and then does Bunting catch a glimpse of his mate Robert Wagner. The men are held in separate sections within the same prison. At the time of writing, Wagner is an inmate in Yatala's B Division.

Wagner's daily routine is much the same as Bunting's, although he lives in a single-person cell. Wagner has spent time as a 'unit worker', dishing out meals and collecting laundry, for which he earns about $40 a week.

Inside B Division, Wagner has befriended another convicted killer, with whom he spends much of his time. Wagner likes to big-note himself and brags of his crimes, often telling horrible tales of murder and talking of his hatred for those he believes are paedophiles. Unlike Bunting, fellow inmates are not frightened of Robert Wagner, and many refer to him with contempt as a 'thick head'.

Mark Haydon also serves his time in Yatala's B Division, but in a different section from Wagner. He has assimilated more willingly into the prison population, but often keeps to himself. As was the case on the outside, Haydon has a reputation for being a quiet man. It is likely that Haydon will be transferred out of Yatala not too far into his sentence, to one of the prisons in South Australia's country areas – perhaps Port Augusta to Adelaide's north, or Mobilong to the west.

As for James Vlassakis – his exact whereabouts remain a closely guarded secret. Having turned on his co-accused and testified against them, Vlassakis is seen as a 'dog', not only by those he spoke against, but by most other inmates. Vlassakis serves his time under a false name, for his own protection. A court order forbids the South Australian media from publishing Vlassakis's location, or even showing his face. Authorities believe that if this were to occur, Vlassakis's life would be in danger.

The term 'serial killer' inspires not only a chilling, fearful reaction in many, but also fascination. Perhaps it is true-life tales dating back as far as Jack the Ripper which have served to arouse people's interest. Perhaps fictional characters like Hannibal Lecter, depicted in the movie *Silence of the Lambs*, have served to glorify the worst kind of human being.

Indeed, much has been written and said about serial killers. In modern times they have been studied, analysed and even allowed to speak for themselves. The US Federal Bureau of Investigation (FBI) classifies a serial killer as a person who murders on at least three occasions, with a break or 'cooling off' period in between. The profile of a 'typical' serial killer is said to be a Caucasian male, aged between eighteen and forty, of above average intelligence and quite often personable, even charming. Contrary to popular belief, they are not freaks who stand out from the crowd. Serial killers are most often blue-collar workers or unemployed, and many have come from dysfunctional childhoods where they were emotionally, physically or sexually abused. Much of this is certainly true of the Snowtown killers, although no killer fits perfectly into the profile. What sets the Snowtown killers apart from so many others is the fact that they formed a murderous group rather than acting alone. This, history tells us, is rare.

However, perhaps the most striking characteristic about John Bunting, Robert Wagner, James Vlassakis and Mark Haydon is their cowardice. Bunting and Wagner preyed on unwitting, vulnerable victims who did not deserve the torture and death inflicted upon them. The pair believed they were on a mission to rid society of paedophiles when, in reality, most of their victims were innocents. These killers overpowered their victims using surprise, and then killed them for their own sadistic pleasure.

For their part, Vlassakis and Haydon were too cowardly to extricate themselves from Bunting's evil circle. Their cowardice allowed the murders to continue. They too have blood on their hands.

The tourists had travelled a long way and, having finally arrived, they could hardly contain their excitement. One of the women in the group used the car's rear-view mirror to fix her hair as her husband fiddled with his camera. The couple and their two friends had taken a stop on their driving holiday which, if their car's registration plates were anything to go by, had brought them from Australia's east coast to the small hamlet of Snowtown. It was a few months since Snowtown had been changed forever by the discovery of eight bodies, in barrels, in the vault of the town's old Bank SA building.

A handful of locals was watching discreetly as the tourists struck a pose outside the building – like dozens before them, they had come to have their photograph taken outside the infamous bank.

Normally Snowtown residents are friendly and helpful, always willing to point a visitor in the right direction. But not today. There were two old bank buildings in Snowtown, and these visitors were posing for photographs outside the wrong one. For once the locals had the last laugh as the insensitive visitors drove out of town.

It was not the worst of what the people of Snowtown have been forced to endure. There were also the tourists who would stop outside the old bank, get down on their hands and knees and sniff under the door, hoping for a whiff of death. There were rats in the ranks, too, like the shopkeeper who tried to cash in on the town's grisly reputation. He began selling sick souvenirs – fridge magnets displaying cartoon drawings of a skeleton in a barrel, along with the words 'I've been to Snowtown – and survived'. Another magnet showed eight barrels with the slogan 'Snowtown SA – You'll have a barrel of fun'. Locals and victims' families were outraged, and the glare of negative publicity was once again on the small town.

For the people of Snowtown there is no escape from the harsh reality of all that has happened there. It is true that only one victim was actually murdered in Snowtown, but it is equally true that it was the place where the killers chose to conceal their evil acts, and the place where the police eventually discovered them. Since then, some Snowtown residents have felt compelled to leave. Others have rallied together to get life back to normal – even make it better. Each of us has our own way of coping with adverse circumstances. But the people of Snowtown, past and present, must hope and anticipate that their home will pass back into anonymity.

One day.

Acknowledgments

Many people helped me tell this story and I owe thanks to them all. In particular I am grateful to Tony Love, Fiona Clark, John Merriman and Sophie Hamley. There are also those who I cannot thank by name. They know who they are.

Most of all I would like to thank my family for their tolerance and support, especially my wife, Melissa.